Magnetic North
The Emerging Poets

Published in 2006
by The Verbal Arts Centre in association with Lagan Press

The Verbal Arts Centre
Stable Lane & Mall Wall
Bishop Street Within
Derry / Londonderry
BT48 6PU
e-mail: info@verbalartscentre.co.uk
web: www.verbalartscentre.co.uk

The Lagan Press
Unit 4
1A Bryson Street
Belfast
BT5 4ES
e-mail: lagan-press@e-books.org.uk
web: lagan-press.org.uk

Supported by
The National Lottery®
through the Arts Council of Northern Ireland

ISBN: 1-898701-60-1

Cover Design by The Verbal Arts Centre
Typeset by The Verbal Arts Centre
Cover Photograph by James Cunningham

Magnetic North
The Emerging Poets

Edited by John Brown

Where do we come to if we follow the compass needle northwards? Irrespective of our starting point… (some) place in the Canadian Arctic, the compass refuses to indicate a distinct direction; the earth's magnetic field points downwards into the ground… Eskimos lived in this region without ever worrying about how special it was - it was European scientists and sailors who found the area interesting, and by the coincidence that the magnetic pole lay where they strove to find the long-sought shortcut to east Asia. But the way was long, in time, distance and knowledge… If we use all the observations from the 1500s until today… the pole has enjoyed a sortie into Canada and is now on its way out into the Arctic ocean again. Geologists find traces of the magnetic field in many minerals (palaeogeomagnetism) and can tell us how the pole has wandered round in the polar region for millions of years, a wandering it will surely continue. Sometimes, however, something remarkable occurs. In fact, the current North Pole is a South Pole in magnetic parlance, this having historical reasons…now and again the two poles change place…The dynamo in the earth's interior is unstable such that on occasion the field weakens, loses its bi-polar character and regenerates with reversed polarity. It is believed that the reversal process takes several thousand years, but some modern opinions suggest a short time. We can only imagine the confusion when the compasses of the world suddenly turn a half circle!

The Road to the Magnetic North Pole, Ultima Thule

Professor Truls Lynne Hansen

… care taken
over positives and negatives.

Device, Colette Bryce

There are others who know what it is
to lose, to hold ideas of north so singularly brutal that the world
might be ice-bound for good.

Remaindermen, Nick Laird

a bearing taken, nothing less than that…

The Road to No Town, Damian Smyth

Acknowledgements

Acknowledgement is due to the poets and the following publishers or journals for permission to reprint poems: Abbey Press (for 10 poems by Adrian Rice from *Impediments* and *The Mason's Tongue*); Black Mountain Press/Flambard Press (for the first 9 poems by Gary Allen from *Languages and Exile*); Bluechrome Publishing (for 'The Book of Invasions' and 'A Chinese Woodcut', by Nigel McLoughlin from *Blood*); Jonathan Cape (for the first 8 poems by Leontia Flynn from *These Days*; by permission of the Random House Group Ltd.); Carcanet Press (for the poems by Sinéad Morrissey from *There Was Fire in Vancouver* and *Between Here and There* and *The State of the Prisons*); Cló Iar-Chonnachta (for the first 8 poems by Gearóid Mac Lochlainn from *Sruth Teangacha / Stream of Tongues*); The Dedalus Press (for the first 8 poems by Chris Agee from *In the New Hampshire Woods* and *First Light*); *The Edinburgh Review* (for 10 poems by Paul Grattan from *The End of Napoleon's Nose*); Gallery Press (for the first 8 poems by Alan Gillis from *Somebody, Somewhere*; 10 poems by Kerry Hardie from *A Furious Place, Cry for the Hot Belly, The Sky Didn't Fall*; 10 poems by Conor O'Callaghan from *The History of Rain, Seatown* and *Fiction* and the first 5 poems by John Hughes from *Negotiations with the Chill Wind* and *The Devil Himself*); *Irish Pages* (for 'North of Nowhere', the final poem by Gary Allen); Lagan Press (for all poems by Jean Bleakney, Deirdre Cartmill, Moyra Donaldson, Dan Eggs, Sam Gardiner, Leon McAuley, Nigel McLoughlin, Pól Ó Muirí, Cherry Smyth, Damian Smyth; for the last 5 poems by John Hughes and the last 7 poems of Sabine Wichert); Open House Festival (for 'To William Kennedy' and 'Johnny Doran' by Gearóid Mac Lochlainn from *Rakish Paddy Blues*); Picador/Macmillan Publishers Ltd. (for 10 poems by Colette Bryce from *The Heel of Bernadette* and *The Full Indian Rope Trick*); *Metre* (for 'Genetics' by Sinéad Morrissey); Phoenix Poetry Pamphlets (for 'It's for You' from *A History of Hello* by Conor O'Callaghan); Salmon Publishing (for Sabine Wichert's 'Of Vistula and Lagan' from *Tin Drum Country* and for 'Irish Summer' and 'The Gate' from *Sharing Darwin*); Summer Palace Press (for 10 poems by Ruth Carr) and Smith/Doorstop Books (for 'Hats', 'Too Dear', 'Aubade', 'At First Our Letters' and 'Cats - A Retrospective' by Paula Cunningham). The editor also wishes to thank Patrick Ramsey for the selection of, and introduction to, the Irish language poems of Pól Ó Muirí.

Contents

Introduction

Magnetic North is an anthology of poetry by twenty-nine emerging poets from the North of Ireland who have made their mark at the start of the twenty-first century. The anthology contains a selection of ten poems by each poet and defines emerging poets as those published in one to four solo volumes of poems. The collection occupies a space, difficult to demarcate, between new poets published in magazines, journals or 'group introductions' and established poets with long-standing or international reputations secured by numerous volumes or repeated selections in anthologies. *Magnetic North*, therefore, features poets who have received major awards or some critical recognition as well as less well-known poets newly published in smaller presses. The anthology, arranged alphabetically, covers poets of all ages but focuses mainly on new work and poems published in the last ten years. The anthology features poets and poetry *"from* the North of Ireland" and the preposition is broadly indicative that birthplace, recurrence of northern subject matter or ongoing writing after the poet took up residence here, are the basis of qualification. Of course all anthologies, no matter how well-defined their parameters, are loosely tied parcels in transit to being re-opened and re-shaped again; this one is no exception. Given the number of practitioners and potential inclusions one cannot claim to be exhaustively prescriptive. Inevitably there are absent qualifiers.

Many poets in *Magnetic North* have lived and written through a particularly troubled period in the North and a period of profound and rapid change in Ireland and the wider world. The title suggests that the North's ongoing, diametrically opposed, self-cancelling currents of sectarianism still generate "lines of departure/ lines of return" (John Montague's phrase) as instincts to belong run counter to the urge for flight - *"Put your hand to the door. Are you coming in or out?"* as Nick Laird puts it. The title also suggests poetry as self-sufficient magnet, ("care/taken over positives and negatives" in Colette Bryce's phrase) which registers hidden energies or "microbes raving in rocks" (Alan Gillis's phrase). Poetry creating new currents, not only taking "bearings" or reading the map. As long as concepts of home ground, however, remain riven by unspoken fault-lines or divided by the borders of the political soap box, then so too does poetry's role in breaking complicit, "sterilised silence" (Deirdre Cartmill's phrase), interrogating the map and crossing borders. Poems like Deirdre Cartmill's 'Cross-Border Express' or John Hughes's 'Pillow Talk' bear witness to this. Poetry, however, not only re-maps, breaks silence or renovates inherited cliché: it charts individual "paths" (Kerry Hardie); imagines "landscape(s) of a private fiction" (Conor O'Callaghan); questions ground's literal ownership ("What ground is mine/if I would govern myself?" Moyra Donaldson asks) and travels not only "*to* or *from* but *in* and *through*" (Damian Smyth).

Alongside poems of place, birthplace or roots - poems from or about the North - there are mobile poems magnetised by other horizons. A crop of poems in this anthology is written through car, bus or aircraft windows; many cross internal, national, international, even stratospheric frontiers. Many poets, as well as Paul Muldoon, have been "a far cry from the Moy" and the result is often bifocal or comparative visions: there's Paul Grattan's Belfast and Vienna; Gary Allen's Antrim and Berlin; Chris Agee's Belfast and Zacatecas; Sam Gardiner's Colorado and Craigavaon; Nick Laird's Warsaw and Donegal; Sinéad Morrissey's Belfast and Japan; Sabine Wichert's Vistula and Lagan. Mairtín Crawford, Leon McAuley and Dan Eggs all navigate between Ulster and outer space. I'm not suggesting poetry as postcard of the exotic over the native but I am suggesting that the *spaces* between people or places are often more important than any single literal or circumscribed location. At the heart of poetic metaphor is the capacity to be in two places at once. Jean Bleakney has talked of "the fascination of what's between"; Sabine Wichert's historical consciousness notes that despite distance the Lagan and Vistula "flow across one latitude"; Leon McAuley's 'Craters' suggests the distance between earth and space is often less than the gap between a married couple in one house just as Leontia Flynn states that "the furthest distances I've travelled/have been between people". Conor O'Callaghan's 'Seatown' is as much about "the eight kilometres from this to open water" as it is about Dundalk. In fact, internal space (within the head or poem) is often the most unfathomable destination of all. Colette Bryce refers to the non-space of idealised love as "Nevers of the mind" just as Sinéad Morrissey's illicit loves are the "unkillable" means "by which our dreams and daily scenes stay separate". In one poem Chris Agee evokes "That time. That place" but alongside this specificity there is his metaphysical space where, after grief, we are "travelling forever into the dark land of eternal light".

This anthology, though, hardly points to the "dark land" or a "Black North" suddenly illuminated by new millennial light. Lunar eclipse as scepticism of "totality", millennia as "a purely human notion" when viewed from Mars, feature more than brand-new dawns. Darkness remains both a felt, elemental or metaphysical presence in John Hughes's work just as in Sabine Wichert's 'Taganrog' a new political dispensation simply amounts to a new economic reality that quenches the eternal flame when the gas bill is not paid. Indeed entropy is a recurrent image in more than one poem here. Perhaps the late 1960s, early 1970s, image of poetry as a "door into the dark" is with us more than we care to acknowledge. Amidst the so-called gleams of fragile, realistic optimism, Alan

Gillis still finds the whole notion of 'progress' (in Belfast) questionable. Recurrent images of "filmic rewind" or "fast forward" suggest that memory or history remain inescapable, often nightmarish, realities from which any imaginative projection or freedom is hard won.

Perhaps, though, the tribal pressures or political expectations of the early Troubles, which compelled poetry to develop self-protective pacts with silence, exile or the cunningly oblique, are now less generally or acutely felt. Certainly, many poems here meet politics head-on: '1981' (Colette Bryce), 'Hats' (Paula Cunningham), 'Backfire' (Mairtín Crawford), '12th October 1994' (Alan Gillis), 'Pillow Talk' (John Hughes), or 'The Remaindermen' (Nick Laird). Certainly the magnetic pull of ancestral or tribal forces (genetics, memories, rituals and buried linguistic codes) as well as the terrible push of actual events, from Hunger Strike to Omagh Bomb, still implicitly, as well as explicitly, shadow many poems. The images in the poetry of the Troubles suggest a complex reality where things were never as bad as they seemed, but worse than they ever were, on television; violence is less regularly, subjectively encountered in daily doses in single lives or poems than it is on the box but when it is, as certain poems suggest, its long-lasting psychological or physical impact are real enough.

If there is more than one type of 'Troubles poem', though, then there is more to poetry from the North than the Troubles. The "dark holy bloody peace" Gearóid MacLochlainn seeks in one poem is not "the sound of no helicopters" but the silence a husband desires when he's been tortured all day by his wife and noisy kids. Kerry Hardie and Conor O'Callaghan - both mainly resident in the South - could hardly be expected, like many adult poets, to dwell forever or long on the North even if it does, infrequently, seep into their work. There are, thankfully, many fine poems in this anthology about other things than typecast themes of Irish politics or Northern angst. Like Paul Durcan, poets simply sometimes think about other things, like Australia for instance. And when they do reflect on the North there is more sanity, humour and humanity than is often found in the political sphere. Take Paula Cunningham's contention that "y-fronts/on the washing line/ (are) the only flags/that ever make you smile...".

There are as many poems here, then, about other things as there are about the North. Poems about the unpredictable or strange, about domesticity or love or life or death (by natural causes) or about the wider universe in which we are enmeshed. Strictly speaking, there are as many poems about how relationships or love frequently defy expectations and seldom run smooth as there are poems poured into the ready-made mould of a genre called 'love poetry'.

There are poems about: adultery and fidelity; hornyness and holiday flings; cinematic romances and porn; domestic violence and saintly ideals; curious affairs between spin dryers and washing machines; annoying men who leave the loo seat up and fastidious women who insist on colourless toilet rolls; sexy men squeezing oranges in kitchens and men who wouldn't pay the price of a postage stamp. There are poems about: boredom bred by familiarity and the new love song in the air; the regret of love's aftermath and the first excitement of meeting a waitress in the cocktail bar. In short, the infinitely unpredictable ways we relate to each other are here; the ways in which we love, fail, dream, suffer or fall apart. And why not? Poetry, after all, is no exam answer to prescribed questions on a hackneyed theme that cooks the books to produce another poem somebody else "made earlier". So here, as well as strange love poems, there are poems about hats, snakeskin stilettos, cats, conservatories, corn circles, Protestant dogs, amusement arcades, a by-pass, a cabinet maker, a sculptor in metal and Crazy Horse. If this collection exerts any magnetic pull whatsoever, it is simply through the whole diverse, unpredictable, range and welter of subject matter or people that crop up when a poet sets to work.

As well as disparate subject matter the anthology seeks to represent diverse genres and poetic shapes. Poetry, even post-Paul Muldoon, remains a self-conscious linguistic medium that shows no sign of slacking in producing poems about poems. Sinéad Morrissey's 'If Words' or Sam Gardiner's 'No Title' use words about words just as Conor O'Callaghan's reflections on "fall" or "hello" or John Hughes's 'The Brains of the Operation' are etymologically powered. Frank Sewell suggests that even one missing letter can trigger whole new meanings just as Paula Cunningham exposes the entire political fall-out that accrues around the pronunciation of the single letter "H". In Gearóid MacLochlainn's work the bilingual tongue is severed but words are still singing. Jean Bleakney looks at ways different dictionaries are made to work. Nick Laird enjoys language that's "layered". The outcast language of graffiti or repeated clichés in a popular song attract Nigel McLoughlin's eye and ear. In fact, the whole strange world of words or language with its infinite patterns, connotations or chaos, is the magnetic core of the book. This anthology, then, proposes to expose readers to new currents within language itself and hopes that this magnetism tempts writers to refashion the current anew.

John Brown, March 2006

Chris Agee

Chris Agee was born in San Francisco in 1956. He attended Harvard
University and, since 1979, has lived in Ireland. He currently lives in
Belfast and teaches at The Open University. Agee wrote a sequence of
poems, *The Sierra de Zacatecas* (Ediciones Papeles Privados, Mexico, 1995),
edited *Scar on the Stone: Contemporary Poetry from Bosnia* (Bloodaxe Books,
1998) and currently edits the journal *Irish Pages*. His poetry collections are
In the New Hampshire Woods (The Dedalus Press, 1992) and *First Light* (The
Dedalus Press, 2003); and a forthcoming poetry collection will be entitled
Next to Nothing.

Agee's poetry draws on a wide range of locales (Mexico, Bosnia and
the Balkans) although Ireland (especially Ulster) and North America
(especially New Hampshire) are recurrent. *In the New Hampshire Woods* is
an ecological volume: plant-, animal- and bird-life are evoked as sources
of wonder, reflection, epiphany and as markers of true worth in an "Age
of Petrol". Underpinning North American and Irish settings is an interest
in language: the "split tongues" of "New England English" and native
American Indian names like "ancient kelp" sit alongside references to
both English and the "peat reek" of Gaelic in Ireland; the salty tang
of Lowell and Melville and the fieldwork of Robert Frost sit alongside
references to Irish writers in English such as W.B. Yeats and Samuel
Beckett. Poetic exemplars such as haiku and early Irish poetry and
the work of painters are directly evoked to suggest natural detail
can symbolise or imply a complete macrocosm akin to the drawings
of Audubon or the photographs of the naturalist Eliot Porter. The
sacramental language of poems like 'Offing' or 'Terminus' suggest Seamus
Heaney as kindred spirit. In *First Light* the poetry engages with public,
historic violence or loss often seen through the oblique lens of nature but
the last two poems in this selection (to be included in *Next to Nothing*)
suggest nature as a lens, filter or indirect symbol for private grief. The
way perspectives alter as we age and the nature of Nature and time are
recurring themes in this work.

Campesino
from The Sierra de Zacatecas

Not far from Don Federico's fountain-piece,
his wizened, weather-bronzed and Oriental features,
his sandals and satchel, his brown jorongo,
broad straw hat and goatee, put me in mind of Basho
in his old age, forsaking his patio and jacaranda,
heading for the country outskirts, for pines, temples,
passes, hamlets, embarking yet again
on the dusty road to a deeper North.

Loon Call

Its black head might surface midafternoon off a dock
of planks weathered gray as wasp's nest: or its call
sound hauntingly across the placid light of Squam

at duskfall, the sky the inside of a seashell: catching me
at a desk in lamplight, back to a screendoor
filled with the endless rattle-shake of summer insects:

standing, gazing upwards in tall meadow grass
shadowed with moonlight, in thrall to the constellations
and the galaxy-mantle of the Milky Way: in ferny birchwoods

aswim with sun-mottle on lichened boulders: reminding me,
like the Möbius of thought turned on itself,
of the life of the moment it mortalizes.

Port of Belfast

Hung on a wall of Calvinist stars,
the moon is a mottled goatskin bodhrán,
a vellum of weathered light
above the fog and frost of Lagan dips.

Offing

That sun, a moon almost: I remember it like a bindi
On the cool brow of a porcelain buddha, a red spot

In the mist of dusk. That place, that microcosmos,
The clean lines of clapboard, the crimson cupola,

Summers in New England, light in August,
What can I say? What can you say of life?

That I was there, that it was here. That place
I first felt its deep offing, that porch I walked from,

The gingerbread of the spartan Cottage,
The shuffleboard, the lawn's two iron deer

Asperged with dew, a Wednesday's sixties line-dance,
Deck rockers under the trestle of stars, gin rummy

In the Sun Room. On down the hill rippling through
To the swans on the Spring House pond,

A teardrop on the brow of the Bluffs,
Deep in cornflowers and Queen Anne's lace.

That place I still return to, fresh as ever,
The clatter of dishes, the old Polish cook

With his broken English and wild eyes,
The waitresses in white, meals *al fresco*

On the laundry landing, *circa* '71.
Sails in the offing, our Shack and psychedelic Barn

Out back towards the wall-quilt and grasses
Sprinkled with cornflowers and Queen Anne's lace.

Out for a break from the dinner din.
In the stillness, the empty Annex, a red disc sinking

Like the buoy of crepuscule. That time. That place
I spent some misspent youth. That porch. That dew.

First Light

One begins not knowing
what the mind will beachcomb from the radiant flux
of things in the intertidal zone, what the combers

have left at first light:
a sawn stump with three worn nodes,
a buoy in wrack, a corncob, a dead ray:

the subtle patinas of the bluffs
beetled by bay and bittersweet,
riddled by the cliff-dwellings of swallows:

dark glistening surf
occasioned by trails of mackerel-cloud:
the vast abstraction

of dry smooth shingle-stones infinitely variable
under foot. Or, finally, brilliant indigo-and-seagreen
under a clearing sky. You have quickstepped thus

in spirit, from stepping-stone to stepping-stone
as if some surefooted Chinese boatman
leaping nimbly athwart junk-to-junk at a mooring -

though unable to say, looking back,
should you ask yourself, how exactly you traversed
that hour's crescent of foaming sand and shingle-bank.

Osterley

It was sometime in June the Tube
stopped one late-bright evening
at Osterley, a few getting out: scuffs, footfalls;

for a bell-clear minute beyond the halt
the drifting Old English air
of Titania and Oberon, meadowsweet and holly

on the embankment; in the compartment, a lone
African and a half dozen others down the aisle
on their way to Heathrow: the Now quickening now

to unalloyed joy, the transmutation
that fills a Space before the doors close hissing,
all of us together, this once, radiant, alone, facing out

towards the stillness and mote-filled light;
as first slowly, then swiftly the train alights
from a now-lustrous, still halt on the daily passage.

Terminus

Whether you are coming or going, Connolly's blotched skylight
Ends in light. Walk the old platform's vanished chessboard

Black-and-white. Before or behind you, the shining filigree
You travelled, or will. Leave all your baggage

In Left Luggage. Pause at the gatekeeper's ticket-punch:
He will wave you in, or out - to, or from

The Morgue's blue door in Amiens Street. Then, light and silence
Where the platform began, or ends -

And even now ends and begins as you move forward
In the compartment of your self-reflection.

Mushrooming

Nothing stills the woods to silence
like the aftermath of rains, the meadow-crickets quenched,
the boughs and saplings of birch and pine

dropping their desultory plops, shining
here and there with sunshafts from parted cloud
whose mottle on moist leaf-litter

is a moss of light. This is the inspired time
the Greeks felt the mystery of Zeus,
the lightning's muse

in the dark labour of fungi. Vicarious as the uprush
of poetry, the delicate caps of mushrooms
thrust through the earth's rot, half-masked by a layer of leaves,

by mossy vestiges of treetrunks
holed by woodpeckers,
birch-logs broken-backed like tumbled pillars of alabaster,

branches fallen in autumn
where Indian pipe sprouts on bark
and a meandering wall is Frost's art

like lichen on the stones of Nineveh. A paradise of phalloi
mushrooming in damp, all named and infused
by the genius of fieldwork,

in the Eden of amateur mycology:
Chanterelle, Thimble-cap, Velvet-footed Pax,
the ochre, Latinate splendour

of *Voluminous Milky*
with its fishstink and profusion of latex:
each under-cap a haven for slugs,

a language all its own,
neither prose nor song,
not animal, yet not quite plant,

their svelte ethereal flesh
and tinges of extraordinary colour
the Zen of life,

a quickening blush of humus
in one-day miracles of the world's design
like haikus in the woodland epic of birth and decay.

Sebald

1944-2001

On and off, I had been musing about vistas
Of simultaneity: the continuum between, say,

In a natural sense, fresh graves in Afghanistan
And the abysmal plain on the Marianas Trench

Lit by the spectral traceries of bioluminescence; or,
In the social, sipping coffee as Srebrenica happened

In waves of twenty-plus. How - at any one time - everything
Is happening in a single world-image like tens of millions

Of words in the Babel of thousands of tongues coexisting
In its archive of consciousness. That interior Friday

In the Year of the Buddhas, it might have happened
As I paused for a moment at a window over Royal Avenue

Or collected my daughter's last photographs amid the sad
Crepuscule of the framing shop. Now, over coffee, reading

Of *seiceamóir and cuileann* in *Trees of Ireland,*
I think of his radiant endings: a last glimpse of the land

now being lost forever and *reaching the town*
as evening began to fall: and hope

His noble German soul and hers in miniature
Are travelling forever into the dark land of eternal light.

Alpine Interlude

When we reached the mountain bog in the saddle
Of Jackson, and saw the heads of thousands
Of cotton sedge trembling and bobbing, letting go

Their fleecy tufts like thistledown in Ireland
Over archipelagos of blackbrown peat sediment -
I thought, after a while, of those days in Kosovo: life

Essential in its passing, its beauty, its tragedy. But first
Pausing long trail minutes, the boy becalmed on
Planks of the bog bridge, seeing mountain cranberry,

Pale laurel, Canada mayflower, windy Appalachian bog
Rimmed by Labrador tea, the sweetness of the moment
Reminded me of Miriam's life, its brevity and softness,

Its summery interlude, its sunniness stretching
Out to the unending dark dwarf balsam fir-trees
And the great universe bowl of the White Mountains

In sheer airy blue outline, the cumuli sailing in
Puffs of snapdragon and Hiroshima… with which,
Nonetheless, in the mind's eye, her time seemed one.

Gary Allen

Gary Allen was born in Ballymena, County Antrim, in 1959. His poems and stories appeared in literary magazines in Ireland, Britain and Holland before the publication of four poetry pamphlets in the 1990s and two poetry collections, *Languages* (Flambard Press/Black Mountain Press, 2002) and *Exile* (The Black Mountain Press, 2004).

In this poetry there are frequent, direct, raw encounters with grief, loss, displacement, cruelty and brutality; these encounters are captured in language characterised by its hard, startling, simplicity and in imagery which reveals an active nihilism, a perseverance wrestling with despair. Many poems explore, through direct concrete images and stark Biblical diction - a language that evokes "their truths, not mine" according to 'Testament' - the negative impact and virulence of the North's inherited religious divisions on the lives of families, the poor and the poet. 'Born Again', for instance, reveals the damaging effects of an obdurate and residual faith where "The Antichrist is real among the broken farm implements". Inherited economic or social divisions are also critically explored. 'The North', for instance, depicts "a great uncle in a wooden tower like a sun-god/watching the bleach-greens white with the linen/for the genteel dining rooms of Boston and Philadelphia". The poetry also deploys the familiar Ulster conceit of the poet as an outsider/craftsman in 'The Cabinet Maker', where a carpenter fashions furniture to create "the simple beauty of a drawer with its own whisper and light movement"; the trope, usually deployed to emphasize creativity, is used here not only to connote the skill of the craftsman but to suggest his tenuous survival in an outhouse of the economic system where he barters for "the odds and ends of rough planks.... from the timber yard". Many poems reveal a deep sympathy for those on the margins of society: the cabinet maker, women, the poor, even the animals in 'North of Nowhere'.

Hymnal

Now I understand, grandfather
the thickening in my fingers and wrists,

and the silence.

Jesus hangs on every wall
to remind us

of sin, and retribution.

Life leaves by the eyes,
my grandmother said

standing over you in resignation.

And I fear too:
the violent single sound of a phone

that rings and stops
in that hour before rising

in a house that is empty with yourself.

Father, what is the meaning of this cross?
let me walk beyond the garden of Gethsemane

and reject the earth, and what is dust
for the assurance of flesh.

First Love

In my house, chairs stood against the windows:
I sweated in fear of the man
with a pillowcase over his head.

The night I walked you home,
lads smoking in the shadows
at the gates of the Parochial House -

Go no farther love, you whispered:

a fool youth, in my rut I would have kissed
you under the famine wall.

And my father sprung up
from the locks he was mending
pressing the blade of a screwdriver to my throat,

his eyes burning like Abraham's.

Love changes nothing, you said,
not even bales of shorn hair,
hillocks of broken teeth.

The Cabinet Maker

And there you are again, the air thick with dust, the smell of fresh cut
wood,
shavings curling up your muscular tattooed arms as you cut true -
with the breaker and the iron just right -
the odds and ends of rough planks bartered from the timber yard.

A pot of melted, foul-smelling animal glue on the hearth
and old canvas awnings from the lorry depot covering the floor.

You are lost in these hours as never before
excelling in your strength and discipline,
intuition, skilful fingers, that something in the eye
that taught to tease out the wood, the grain, the precise cut

as you slot dovetail, bevel with a spokeshave and file
and with the small knife you fashioned from the iron in the shipyard

inwardly carve the bone-hard handle for a cabinet door,
consoles for shelves, little catches -
the simple beauty of a drawer with its own whisper and light movement.

The Broiler House

She is the fresh one
at the end of this line

of worn-out women with podgy faces
and brawny arms

hands viscid
with guts, giblets, membranes.

The heavy-set man behind them
in the blood-flecked apron
is mouthing a dirty joke,

cleaver-raping moribund meat,
pink and gaping like an open mouth.

This is the beginning of seven children
and the loss of small things -

girlhood, innocence, church on Sunday,
the sanctity of flesh.

Languages

And this is your first real sense of freedom,
flying down the Alp passes on your Norton into Italy
the flight jacket zipped tight against the wind -
those late-night letters becoming harder to scribble
knowing how heavy every word became in their hands.

The virtues of a good upbringing and self-respect
that your father tried to impart on that last walk along Tremadog Bay,
as you stared at the creased skin on his face and neck
tattooed blue by years at the coalface,
are the very things you hurled your youth against
in the bars and brothels of postwar Berlin.

Visits back to the terraced house in Porthmadog becoming rarer
your dress uniform making you awkward among friends
how you itched to get overseas again
away from uncles, aunts, the solemn chapel Sundays
the rain falling off slates, shop signs, doorways
like the haemorrhaging hours of childhood -
tracing routes along the marble fireplace.

And you could never understand how a man who spent his life in mines
could waste hours studying the texts of your old school grammars -
what Welsh you had flattened out to control-tower monotone
as you talked down combat aircraft over German skies.

His shape still living in the old coat hanging behind the bedroom door,
photographs of himself outside pits in the Rhondda during the forties
scattered with pictures of you on the dresser,
and all the postcards you forgot sending while on leave across Europe.

Born Again

Here are the moon children,
hair the colour of barleycorn and bowl-cut round,
quaint neighbours in the townland of Carnalbanagh.

In puzzlement, they stand aloof in the schoolyard
holding hands, like paper dolls in homemade frocks -
their schoolwork always meticulous, if heavy with God.

The Antichrist is real among the broken farm implements,
the shreds of torn dress blowing in the hawthorns -
always at the elbow, he walks with Mass-goers.

In summer they hold baskets of washing for their mother to hang
and Jacob is a small thing, all day wrestling in the bottom meadow
the land is full of those who have turned from the Word.

They look at the antics of uncles, aunts, and cousins
with sadness in their large blue eyes,
who balk at grace round the table, unwashed in the blood of the lamb.

God is rather like their father - not to be crossed,
a dry love, silent and exact:
and sometimes at night, this tall house crashes in sin.

Testament

It was their truth, not mine
though I never questioned what was inbred,
an accepted and natural inevitability - like death.

That they were good men, I had no doubt,
hard-working, sometimes to the exclusion of all else,
yet I was slow to see the fault lines that was contradiction.

My great uncle, a guarded cobbler, mouth full of tacks,
cross-legged at the workshop window,
neither drank nor smoked, yet fathered three illegitimate children.

And my grandfather, whose everyday speech was biblical.
eschewing all that was underhand or false,
dutifully used his blockhammer like an ass's jawbone
on the unemployed Catholics outside the shipyard gate.

Their laws were clear, if not always just,
and need not be spoken to elicit fear,
like Jesus, who hung in every room,
they could see wrongdoing in a child's face.

And God spoke to them, a voice loud as their own,
never to the women, whose bodies harboured sin
(my cousin still bears the strap scars on her back
when he caught her playing with the iron poker).

My grandmother made us kneel and pray
while he was dying in the room above,
then took each of us in turn to pay our last respects.

And although the curtains were drawn on the living world,
with a child's horror I could clearly see
the black blood clotted in each nostril.

At her bidding, I kissed his parchment head
and with fascinated profanity, I whispered
into his cottonwool-plugged ear. Your God is dead.

The War Zone

And all the public houses had grills:
speak easy, love

for in this park
there has been many executions

the sound of our hearts thumping
like the giant pistons in an engine room.

These are strap marks on my back,
the map your lips read -

a father crying, *You have shamed me.*

Listen love, to bin-lids on paving-stones -
they are warning us.

It is the sinful parts of our youth
they want to destroy -

the knife that cuts away manhood,
the burning tar that scars face and breast,

and the warm smell of animal dung
as we betray each other

Walls

Sometimes we make lives so small
we aspire to nothing
and are grateful:

up here it is always Sunday

and the crack of my hammer disturbing the quiet
setting off crows

picking over a sheep carcass
in the valley.

And I believe too,
that single-mindedness is the only truth

for everything is focused to the same end
and becomes narrowed in time

like the perspective
of this line of fencing posts.

The days are short:
I have cut stone from the quarry below
in a bitter season

numb fingers breaking bread
in the graveyard at Racavan -
sad lost souls,

and the wind, bringing down mountain loneliness
to a man who finds love repulsive,
the earth not desolate enough.

North of Nowhere

These are cows that move dumbly
across the gorse and thistles,

but they could be human

alive in their own stream of piss
their inattention to what surrounds them:

in that shed over there I stretched gut
ten hours in salted water

hands ballooning - the bloated maggoty carcass
of one who got too close to the river,
the child who left us to swim the floods.

These beasts are giant
munching the car-lights on the motorway
striding the black slated roofs of the housing estate.

Where do cows go to sleep at night mister?
my ma says standing in fields

have you ever seen a bull's balls,

or a pit-bull snapping a herd
into the barbed wire entanglements round the substation,

or the great staring eye
before the bolt is shot?

I stand outside, covered in shit and blood
and like a fool I pray.

What are cows used for?
Handbags, belts, shoes -

and sometimes, like humans, they look at the moon.

Jean Bleakney

Jean Bleakney was born in Newry, Co Down, in 1956. She was educated at Queen's University in Belfast where she studied Biochemistry. She currently works in a garden centre in Belfast. Her two collections of poetry are *The Ripple Tank Experiment* (Lagan Press, 1999) and *The Poet's Ivy* (Lagan Press, 2003).

In these poems human relationships, in all their manifestations and changing moods, are a central concern. Metaphors drawn from gardening, botany or weather offer an oblique lens and camouflage for playful and serious explorations of how we interact or yield symbols for the Troubles as in 'Mock Orange' or 'Postcard'. Flowers and plants are double-edged metaphors in poems which advise: "Take this botanical advice/*Buttercups are loaded dice.*" The density and concentration of metaphors drawn from fields such as gardening or science, then, are a distinguishing feature of this work. The love poems vary from the wryly mischievous or ironic to the apparently fatalistic and wistfully accepting; this tonal range means that the metre and rhyme of light verse and the cadence of the short lyric are brought into play; there are echoes of diverse poetic exemplars such as Louis MacNeice and Wendy Cope but the poet is in thrall to no one and her poetry itself warns against easy classifications of influence as a "parlour game". Poems straddle, elude and subvert the very expectations of the traditional forms they evoke to bring literary traditions under unexpected, experimental pressures. In 'Afterwards', for instance, Thomas Hardy's nature poem, full of activity, is turned inside out to become a poem about housework full of entropy, written by an urban woman/poet at the turn of another new century. Even the poet's own dictionary, as revealed in one poem, is really between an old and a latest edition; the choice of language is the poet's own, driven by the needs of the individual poem but often "inclined to stray/ towards the weird, the lovely, and the risqué…"

Postcard
Sunday 16th August 1998

It's been the wettest summer here in years.
As suntans fade away and tourists leave,
we count the sun among the disappeared.

The seaside towns are stacked with souvenirs
that won't sell now. And still we can't believe
how bad it's been, the worst we've had in years

- no notion of the 'good day' perseveres.
We give the nod to autumn for reprieve
and count our hopes among the disappeared.

In rain that is commensurate with tears
another generation learns to grieve.
On this, the hardest summer here in years,
we count the maimed. We name the disappeared.

The Physics of a Marriage

Well matched, they say of us. To me it's clear
that symmetry was just the half of it.
Same wavelength I suppose. Yes darling, we're
the ripple tank experiment that worked
and even though the floor got soaked
the pattern somehow held. We knew it would.
Those corrugations clinched. But oh the debt
to synchronicity and amplitude.

A Woman of Our Times

I wish you wouldn't look at me
as if to say *It's a tip, this place.*
There must be six weeks' Sunday papers
on that sofa. You couldn't find room
to butter a slice of bread…
you wouldn't want to put
a slice of bread on that worktop.
Would you ever considering hoovering?
I wish you'd would think before you look.

I wish you'd BLINK instead and see
A Woman of Our Times
- a dedicated scientist
employing all of her resources
in the absence of outside funding
- a physicist painstakingly unravelling
the Second Law of Thermodynamics;
almost touching base in Chaos Theory
- a woman up to her eyes in entropy.

Fidelity, Fidelity

The ever-tilting monorail of love
demands a sense of balance. It can take
a weather eye and faith in gyroscopes
not to panic, not to pull the brake.

When never-met horizons steal the eye,
familiar stations blur. Desire deletes
embankments, viaducts and fallow fields.
The window mists with gathering deceits.

Get off the train. Discover the illusion
was parallax - the powerful undertow
that drains away the near-to-middle distance
but steadies skylines. Only then you'll know

how destinations often disappoint.
The view can pale. The sun might never shine.
Hearts are mostly safest when they hold
a season ticket for the local line.

Afterwards
after Hardy

When I'm gone - when they gather round and see the grey
Gradation up the curtains, the mugs' brown rings,
The dust, the clutter, the tacky vinyl - will the neighbours say
'She was a woman who never noticed such things'?

Summer Love Was Ever Thus...

like roadside grasses, feathered into bloom,
recoiling from the strangeness of a car
but lunging at its wake - those hapless plumes
seed constellations in the melting tar.

Dangerous Driving

I clocked up 60,000 miles
during your years away
in the city of cyclists;
miles as empty as oceans,
knowing that around no corner
across no central reservation
could I glimpse you driving
that modest little hatchback.

You called one day and said
I'm home, I'll get in touch.
You only lingered long enough
to show me your new car -
updated modest little hatchback;
deeper shade of blue.
Take care and call me soon
was all that I could manage.
I watched you drive off
into weeks and months,
God help me, years of no word.

I know that I should ring or write
but phones are lightning conductors;
and the sudden desperation of a letter,
like overtaking on a bend,
is more than I dare...

You live on my side of town. Your house
is in a cul-de-sac (off a cul-de-sac)
with a bitch of a turning circle
that makes epics of arrivals.
So I trawl the suburbs
never finding fifth gear;
never needing full beam.

How dangerous my driving has become
since your return. By day I scan for indigo.
By night I filter numberplates
sideswiped from the dazzle.
A sticky clutch and dicey brakes say
it's time to trade in. But I'm afraid to.

I'm holding out for the day
that you drive toward me,
unseen, out of a blinding evening sun;
that you might recognize
this now rare battered saloon
- that you might remember...

My dear, we are closing on the hour
when we will meet, fatherless,
at the crossroads of the cemetery.
There, in an awkward clinch of grief,
we will know - you and I -
how prodigal we've been
with miles and years.

Lunar Eclipse Viewed from Conservatory

Prepared to be 'gobsmacked', or 'humbled with awe',
I stationed myself near the double-glazed door:
armchair by the heater, a stool for my feet
and Henry Mancini (*swoon, swoon*) on REPEAT.

Totality came and totality went
and yes, it looked different, though, in the event,
not 'blood soaked' nor 'roseate'. As I recall
(but don't quote me): translucent, a sucked brandy ball.

On Seeing a Poet at the Filling Station

I'd always thought that poets are the driven,
who get the bus and measure time in streets,
and choose to view, or not to view, the close-ups
a forty-mile-an-hour blur deletes.
Drivers take wide-angled, distance views.
They never feel the gradient of camber
and seldom have to size the pavement's drop
where water lies and fretted petals gather.

Yet step-by-step means dog dirt in the grooves
and, just as visceral, the bus lane judder;
and facing up to hail or summer lows
while those behind the wheel are under cover.
So, on reflection… sober, level-headed
is the poet who can operate, unleaded.

Looking Up

I'm stuck in that difficult transition
between a loved old dictionary and its latest edition;
and though I'm grateful to be up to speed
on fractals and superhighways, I feel the need
to mourn the loss of all those headers
elevated by chance and typesetters.
There they sat, smug as teachers' pets
- signposts for slow learners - and yet
for all their boldness, those eyecatchers
were only 'befores' or 'afters'
- a litany of never-quite-the-right words,
thrown down like first-round discards.
Which is not to say they weren't time wasters,
sometimes, lingered over like found newspapers.
Farewell then, **dunk, masturbate** and **regret...**
now fallen back into the proletariat.
The whole distracting business starts again
with **kickie-wickie, miscible** and **sex** (hyphen)
- reassuringly disparate headlines
from a new dictionary that, straight-faced, defines
'tomorrow' as 'the day after today'.
No wonder the eye's inclined to stray
towards the weird, the lovely, and the risqué...
whence meaning, sometimes. Sometimes poetry.

Colette Bryce

Colette Bryce was born in Derry in 1970. She studied English Literature and Sociology at St Mary's College, Twickenham. Twelve poems by the poet were included in *Anvil New Poets 2* (1995). She has two poetry collections, *The Heel of Bernadette* (Picador, 2000) and *The Full Indian Rope Trick* (Picador, 2004), currently holds a Fellowship in Creative Writing from the Scottish Arts Council and the University of Dundee and is based in Dundee.

Colette Bryce's poetry favours the short lyric driven by rhythm, rhyme and sinuous syntax. The poetry uses children's chants, street rhyme, folk song, advertising jingle or prayer; it evokes the short lyrics of William Blake or the sombre music of Philip Larkin but the real inner music and visual wit is the poet's own. Poems explore growing up amidst Northern Ireland's divisions and sectarian fissures. Inner borders are also examined: the borders between childhood and adulthood, said and unsaid, distance and closeness, secular world and sacred word, the ordinary and surreal image. Sound and rhythm motor a flexible variety of forms; these songs of innocence and experience even encompass opposing views so that adults, for instance, who endure and conform can appear as both heroes or as despicable traitors of childhood's instincts. Poems appear deceptively simple but the speed and rhythm of lyrical, often first person, narratives allow for slippages, deliberate ambiguities and ventriloquisms which keep dramatic changes of voice and multiple readings alive. The poems intrigue and unsettle by frustrating closure promised in their rhythm, by inhabiting shifting borderlands (spaces between and within people) while using precise and sharply defined, concrete images and nouns to depict this. The result is sinuous verse. Constantly evolving rhythms render and relinquish the world by making it readable in, and resistant to, language simultaneously. In 'Pieces' where this technique is pushed to its absolute limit, solid nouns, an inventory of objects, are arranged into the coherent, alliterative music and rhyme demanded by the poem while still remaining stubbornly fragmented - refusing reassembly into coherent order or mending in the world. The result is startling: both a singing line and a domestic Guernica - delivered at one and the same time.

Line,

you were drawn in the voice of my mother;
not past Breslin's, don't step over.
Saturday border, breach in the slabs,
creep to the right, Line,
sidelong, crab,

cut up the tarmac, sunder the flowers,
drop like an anchor,
land in The Moor as a stringball
ravelling under the traffic,
up, you're the guttering scaling McCafferty's,

maze through the slating,
dive from sight and down into history, Line,
take flight in the chase of the fences,
leap the streets
where lines will meet you, race you, lead

you into the criss-crossed heart of the city
of lines for the glory, lines for the pity.

Break

Soldier boy, dark and tall, sat for a rest
on Crumlish's wall. *Come on over.*

Look at my Miraculous Medal.
Let me punch your bulletproof vest. *Go on, try.*

The gun on your knees is blackened metal.
Here's the place where the bullets sleep.

Here's the catch and here's the trigger.
Let me look through the eye.

Soldier, you sent me for cigs but a woman
came back and threw the money in your face.

I watch you backtrack, alter, cover
your range of vision, shoulder to shoulder.

The Pieces

Transit van, fireguard, canvas,
standard lamp, a wintered lake,
art room, lips, a baby bath,
two hands, a knife, a wedding cake,

pavement, sandals, banister,
champagne, rucksack, bus stop, ear,
sunset, ceiling, knee sock, corner,
forehead, skyline, sofa, car,

Santa Claus, cartoon, carnations,
Easter egg, Communion veil,
ocean, windows, LPs, onions,
waving painted fingernails,

breast, a mattress, transit van,
witch's cat, a threshold, ash,
eyebrow, paint-brush, bed sheet, snow-man,
foot, balloon, a black moustache,

forearm, ribbons, dinner plates,
turpentine, baptismal font,
cashpoint, paper party hats,
pumpkin, yellow plastic phone,

ambulance, red-brick houses,
pinafore, the Isle of Skye,
sand, a priest, a pair of glasses,
swimsuit, tinsel, altar, thigh.

Heroes

I used to side with suicides,
the solemn mail of morning tides,
hopeless railroad valentines,
the sullen youths or laughing brides
in photographs, in books, in black and white.
I used to think them heroes, brave and wise.
It's strange the way the years adjust the eyes,
the mind, to meet us, further down the line,
with heroes of another kind.

The ones that stopped, stepped back, slowed down,
have borne the time in minutes, hours,
have known the line but somehow carried on.
The girl with swimming vision
who picked up the phone.
And this man descending the xylophone
steps from the bridge, on this worn afternoon,
who knows, may clear the journey home,
take his coat off, put the kettle on.

Young

Loose stacks of cassettes collapse
to the slam of the door behind us.
We take the stairs
in twos and threes,

we don't know where we might be
this time next year,
but meanwhile,
we apply to the future in lunch-breaks;

taste the possibility, the sweet adhesive
strip of A4 envelopes on tongues,
punch the day and run
to post, to home, and out.

We eye each other up as future lovers;
our faces smooth as blank maps
of undiscovered countries,
where only we might go.

We mean to go, we thumb the guides,
we spin the globe and halt it
at Calcutta, then Alaska, now Japan,
and plan. Imagine.

Not for us the paper lanterns of remember,
but the hard bright bulbs of sheer want.
We reminisce at length
about the future, which is better;

we harbour it in our hearts
like a terrible crush. We laugh
and drink to this in rented rooms.
We think Not this, but older, elsewhere, soon.

Song of the Vagrant
after the Spanish

I have no ties here, not even you
you who gave me your kiss when a kiss
could have killed me.
I survived.
These streets will lead to highways, water, sky.

I will see other cities through other eyes.
Another capricious mouth may kiss,
may kill me.
This is lies.
I will walk these streets repeated; tethered, tied.

Nevers

Passions never spoken,
never broken but preserved,
never layered under marriages
or burnt to dust by fast affairs
are saints to us,

the sacred ones,
bodily enshrined
to lie in state like Bernadette
at Nevers of the mind;
amazing, garlanded and fair.

Older, at the inkling
of an accent or a smile,
we travel there.

1981

A makeshift notice in the square
says it with numbers, each day higher.
North of here, in a maze of cells,
a man cowers, says it with hunger,
skin, bone, wrought to a bare
statement. Waiting, there are others.

Days give on to days; we stall
in twos and threes in the town centre,
talk it over, say it with anger,
What's the news? It's no better.
Headlines on the evening paper
spell it out in huge letters.

Over graves and funeral cars
the vast bays of colour say it
with flowers, flowers everywhere;
heads are bowed, as mute as theirs,
that will find a voice in the darker hours,
say it with stones, say it with fire.

The Full Indian Rope Trick

There was no secret
murmured down through a long line
of elect; no dark fakir, no flutter
of notes from a pipe,
no proof, no footage of it -
but I did it,

Guildhall Square, noon,
in front of everyone.
There were walls, bells, passers-by;
then a rope, thrown, caught by the sky
and me, young, up and away,
goodbye.

Goodbye, goodbye.
Thin air. First try.
A crowd hushed, squinting eyes
at a full sun. There
on the stones
the slack weight of a rope

coiled in a crate, a braid
eighteen summers long,
and me -
I'm long gone,
my one-off trick
unique, unequalled since.

And what would I tell them
given the chance?
It was painful; it took years.
I'm my own witness,
guardian of the fact
that I'm still here.

+

Through the cabin window's haze
we watch the black shadow of our plane
free itself from the undercarriage,
separate, then fall away.

With it falls the sunlit runway,
grids of crops and reservoirs, then all
the scattered glitter of a city
falls, the tattered coastline of a country

plunges out of view.
And just when you might expect to see
the globe in brilliant clarity,
cloud fills the tiny screen

and we, who haven't taken off
at all, wait, seatbelts on,
for the world to turn and return to us
as it always does, sooner or later,

to fix itself to the craft again
at a point marked with the shadow of a plane,
pencilled now on a runway, growing
larger under Irish rain.

Ruth Carr

Ruth Carr was born in Belfast in 1953. She was awarded a bursary from Arlen House, Dublin, for work of promise in 1982 but did not publish her first collection until 1999 (*There is a House*, Summer Palace Press). In the eighties she wrote and staged a Revue entitled *Monroe, Page Three, the Kitchen Sink and Me* and edited the first anthology of women writers to come out of the North, *The Female Line* (Northern Ireland Women's Rights Movement, 1985). She also co-edited *HU, The Honest Ulsterman* poetry magazine for a number of years and compiled the section on contemporary women's fiction for the *Field Day Anthology* IV/V. Her poems have been published in anthologies such as *Word of Mouth* (Blackstaff, 1998) - which has recently been translated into Russian, *A Conversation Piece* (Abbey Press, 2002) and *The Backyards of Heaven* (2003). She works as an associate lecturer in adult education.

Ruth Carr's poetry seeks compassionate "correspondence" with other lives; intimate, sometimes familial, poems laced with deft, surprising metaphors explore relationships between the generations and sexes as well as societal issues. Relationships between parent and child and between wife and husband are central in Carr's poetry; her voice articulates the history and reality of both individual and collective female experience. Poems such as 'Hanging Tree', 'Parity', 'Our Lady' and 'Sukina' explore the way in which female voices are often endangered or marginalised by injustice, cruelty or silence. The imagery in the poems cuts through the slow, frequently dulling habits of domesticity or intimacy to inject new, symbolic life into overlooked or everyday objects often taken for granted (cups, baths, bowls or tables); conversely, the wild is sometimes tamed in surprising ways as in 'Hokkaido'. The poetry's delicate combination of lyrical immediacy and wry reflection makes new the known, makes familiar the unknown, as poems "refract in a rainbow all (the poet knows)/about love, about correspondence."

Family Snap

This is the daddy in a disguise
unknown in a suit but the same limpid eyes.
Overtime pays for coats and shoes
bread he wins and tales they lose.

This is the brother in Sunday best
who stands up tall like a knight on a quest.
Leaving behind his imaginary friend
he wears a school tie and stares straight at the lens.

This is the sister in home-made dress
with turned-in toes and matchstick legs.
Her feet face the front but her body swings round
watching a shadow creep over the ground.

This is the holiday out of the sun
caught in bright spell by the one
uniting three figures who shyly stand
hand in unfamiliar hand.

Red Riding Hood's Mother

I am cleaning my daughter's shoes last thing at night
the house to myself as I gently press
my fingers into the toe of no glass slipper -
these days Dr Marten's the fitting shoe
for a young girl's foot.

I am watching the polish glide on with the guilt
rubbing what isn't a kindness into the heel,
only this far can I go -
wax melting on contact, proofing the steps
of one whose feet I would dress
in anemones from the wood.

On Ice

You splashed about in the bath
with our daughter,
I neglected to scrub your back
and made dishwashing sounds
in the kitchen.

You left
silently
a watermark of love on her brow;

I pulled the plug
and watched our bitter-sweet waters
gurgle away,
not even a tidemark
of what had once been warm and moving.

Just one giant
glacial field
of porcelain white.

Remnant

The smell of you that I carry
fragile as the moth on my old winter coat.

The smell that disintegrates
at the mildest inquiry into the state of us.

The smell that I quarry
in the recess of remembered places

the cave of your arms
the cup of your palm
the nape of your mythical neck.

The smell of you that cuts me adrift
on cedarwood and water
uncontainable as the sea.

In Hokkaido

In Hokkaido
the Japanese crane
in long black stockings and feather boa
picks her way through dancing snow
now you see her
now you don't.

Symbol of happiness
perched on stilts
like tentative thoughts of summer
she persists
where bears are baited in concrete pits
in Hokkaido

Parity

men lead lives of quiet desperation
                    H.D. Thoreau

In this land
where the law is like a public bar
with no toilet -
the men pissing out the back yard -
women lead lives
of even quieter desperation.

Our Lady

Our Lady, dispossessed
on some alpine ice-cap
would not look out of place
in ski-pants, zipping
down virgin slopes
to the sound of music.

But wait for her second
coming round the mountain -
the icon-shattering thaw.
Our immaculate image, white-iced
and frosted for two thousand years,
might melt to nothing more divine
than a seething woman, cheated
out of sex and a son in his prime.

Along the Red Road

I come to a place
in the palm of my hand
where the road runs out
and there is nothing but rock.

Only my fingers,
wrapped around the need
to pass through walls
inside the heart
can find an opening,
let the stone roll.

No messiah,
white-skinned or black
can lift me up from Wounded Knee.
I hold or I release my own Drumcree.

Hanging Tree

In the featherless heart of a night plucked bare
I hear what the crows have been calling
for hundreds of years;
I hear with an unstopped ear:
Caught in the tree, caught in the tree,
tongue of a woman with healing spells,
calling the wind, calling the moon,
calling on me to peck her free.

Sukina

She smiles so sweetly from the photograph.
Headlines next to *Thatcher No Lame Duck*
and *Dubcek's Human Face.*

She wouldn't spell her name right, five years bold.
Daddy's savage lesson with a rule
and plastic tubing and his fists -

and still to come the kettle flex and plug.
He tipped her in the bath, he slapped her back
with salt, he beat her to a pulp.

She died of pain
and shock
and sheer exhaustion.

Daddy No Lame Duck
Sukina's Human Face
Tomorrow someone else will take her place.

Deirdre Cartmill

Deirdre Cartmill was born in Moy, County Tyrone, in 1967. She studied Electronic Engineering and received an M.A. in Creative Writing from Queen's University, Belfast. Her first collection of poems was entitled *Midnight Solo* (Lagan Press, 2004). She currently lives in Belfast, where she works as a television script editor for the BBC.

Deirdre Cartmill's poems explore relationships or measure distance from the position of a moment when the poet is alone confronting loss or the memory of a shared past. Wry, ironic and detached, the poems still hit an intensely human note; they balance both thought and feeling. The poems deploy a great variety of different forms - the villanelle, sonnet, the longer poem sequence and short lyric. A poet born into the Troubles, Cartmill puts new pressures on the clichés and claustrophobia of inherited political legacies of the North. In a so-called post-ceasefire society she appears both wary of those who try to delete individual and communal history for the sake of a sugared normality as well as of those who seek to use history to perpetuate tainted tribal patterns inherited from a communal past that ignores individual fractures and pain. The poetry is still shadowed by "skeletons of border checkpoints", still living with a long-standing chronological sense of the North - as one poem suggests using Stewart Parker's words - as "a place of perpetual breakdown". While the poems point to our absolute and uncircumscribed uniqueness as individuals, each with our own story, they also bear witness to the weight of family or communal histories which claim us. The poetry interrogates contemporary communal concerns: the current political limbo of Northern Ireland; the cross-border suspicions or clichés; the impact of the loss of the "adreneline rush" of the Troubles; the "sterilised silence" of 'The Moy Made Me' where "resurrection" is still awaited and the way in which we are part of another bigger, tribal story which stakes its claim through genetics, styles (of knitted jumpers) and the forensics or rituals of death. There is a subtle humour in this poetry too though, reminders that an old century may well, ironically, open into a new where "gable Messiahs speak truth/ - the future is ours."

The Moy Made Me
after Paul Muldoon

Here in the heart
of the murder triangle
we carried our dead
like talismans,
turned our rosary beads,
invoked the Holy Trinity.

Year after year
the ceasefires came
and went, like deadwood in the river,
beaten back, carried downstream.
The skulking water
earned its black name.

That hill on the far shore
is a burial mound.
The lush grass succours
bones. The ground
rouses skeletons as ciphers
and the ghosts have found

their way under our skin.
They bleed through us
and we can't begin
to start again, to loose
ourselves from the sins
of our bloodlines

when we still hunger
for the adrenaline rush
of death, for martyrs
to prove it wasn't pointless.
A muted prayer
and a funeral hush

are all we've ever known.
We hide our shame
like guns under floorboards,
claim to be blameless
but subsist in shadow,
whisper the names

of the dead. Who would dance
with us? Our throats are cut
and our tongues
are buried with our bullets
in sterilised silence,
awaiting resurrection.

Cross-Border Express

The windows shudder as we stagger past
fields burnt yellow after the harvest,
a Union Jack carved on a rock face,
the skeleton of the border checkpoint,
CCTV, a watchtower on an overhang.
We pass through a gap of stone and heather,
cross that imaginary line and I feel a pang
for home although half my kin were reared here.
I'm a curio. They come to see
each slur carved into my skull and limbs,
my bloated eyes, my shattered knees,
the roll call tattooed on my skin.
They bless themselves and sing a hymn
for the half-breed, branded as suspect and victim.

Invocation

They want me to talk about the heather,
the berries bleeding into the verges,
the Mournes humped against the thunder;
to name our own - nightshade, bog oak,
horsetails, poppies, tansies, spleenwort

and deny that indistinct feeling
that hangs like yesterday's smoke;
to wait for smashed windows and a gulder,
to know my belonging is short-term,
to listen to them talk about the weather.

In a Time of Peace

They've deleted what I said.
I didn't hawk their new vision.
They say history is dead,

it's time I dropped my heady
principles, embraced their tradition.
They've deleted what I said,

rewritten it and signed
it in my name. Their evangelists
say history is dead,

I must be bled until I'm cleansed,
until I follow their catechism.
They've deleted what I said

and now say none of it happened,
that I imagined the divisions
and now history is dead

I must be reborn. Incensed,
I screamed at anyone who'd listen
so they've deleted what I said,
yet they say history is dead.

Someone Else's Story

is knit into my skin.
I have tried to undo the stitches
but my face will always place me;

like a fisherman's geansaí
where each knit, purl and loop
forms the mark of a village,

they have rendered their pattern on me
and even in death they will have me.

First Aid in English Class Reader Book E

The inside cover bears my uncle's name,
alongside doodles of bearded moonmen.
You'd read us stories of sea dogs, treasure,
Jonah in the belly of the whale.

When you worked the overnight shift
I'd sneak the book from your top drawer,
lose myself in Arabian nights,
fall asleep to New World folklore.

Over the years you stuffed its pages
with cuttings from your boxing in '59,
bowls wins, marathons, dinner dances.
I keep it wrapped in a plastic bag

but sometimes I shuffle through your photos,
revision notes, tickets, memorial cards,
a napkin from the Benner Hotel, Tralee
- from your honeymoon perhaps?

A violation, I know. I'm searching for signs
- a letter I wrote you when I was five,
a shot of me smiling on a tricycle,
or snuggled in a pram at Dublin Zoo.

I flick through your black-and-white adventures
as you push my mother on a swing,
feed a crow perched on your shoulder,
help John Pat stack hay.

I never rearrange the entries
in this, your life's work of art
slotted haphazardly between blue covers.
I linger over each encryption

in the treasure map you've left me,
as if I could somehow open the pages
in a hidden sequence and unlock
the path that leads to you, now.

I'll always see you as Tom Sawyer,
ducking and diving through these words,
whooping through stories within stories.
I want to sneak up on you one last time

but you're too sleekit and I can't capture
the boy with the cardigan zipped up to his smile,
the man afraid to hold his first-born,
the arseways way you held my hand.

Take Off
i.m. Dad

Rain slabbers across the windows as we turn
on Runway 22, accelerate and lift
into the air above the taciturn
streets and the shipyard drenched in mist.

My ears pop as we drift through candyfloss,
rise from the cotton sea into a sky
the colour of your eyes and mine. As we cruise,
my thoughts freefall and I imagine I hear you sighing

as you mull over your cryptic crossword:
six across - shuffle a languid anger.
You taught me to look upwards, see further
when we stood by the fence at Dublin airport,

watching the planes pass into the grey.
Now I know they crash through to the light.
I love it up here where the streets look so tiny
I could sweep them into my fist

and I could walk on clouds to the horizon
and beyond. Would I find you there, smiling
down on me as I travel so fast
I look as if I'm standing still?

Kitty Snow's

You sink into the hills like a child's hand
snuggling into its mother's palm.

The silence you wear like a glove
can't protect me from the cold caw of crows,
sheep bleating like gurning children,
the burble from your overgrown well.

You peek at the Mournes through a fan of mist,
throw open your gates provocatively,
reluctant to admit
you're a hundred-and-fifty years old.

Flies buzz round your trap,
horseless now,
both of us abandoned with nowhere to go.

The craggy hills sprout stones like warts,
a starling carries a worm to its nest,
and I rest by your hearth, like a seanachaí

destined to repeat the stories written
in the stored up warmth of your walls.

Kitty Snow's is a cottage in Co. Down where the poet lived from 1998-1999.

One Small Step

We are the generation who diss
the moon walk as quaint history.
We look through Hubble's lens,
to the bounds of our universe.
We are neutrons freed from orbit,
decaying through light years,
so we turn inwards, look to spirit,
Buddha, earthmother. We hum our *ohms*,
probe new bounds with our sonar,
so we can know ourselves
as the still-burning cinders of a star-fire.

Slan Abhaile

I

I imagine an exotic stranger smoking Dunhill,
not you on your knees in a County Armagh field
snipping strawberry stems with your thumbnail.
You reach your hand in to ease back the leaves
but it's catapulted back by a nettle sting.
I have been there when bubble-wrap blisters
burn on your skin, when the rain blows in
and you cling like a limpet. You show me a picture
of the daughter you left behind.
Your stained hand leaves a welt under your eye.

II

I dreamt of these fields when I stayed
in a country where the stars were bullet holes
and the sky was a map of an unknown place.
I felt as awkward as a Millie shuffling in Scholls.
I took a wrong turn into a piss-stinking alley,
hissed back at a tomcat - two savages
vying for space in a cramped city
that would have ousted us. Trying to be savvy
I slunk back to the sodium glare
and a curse from a passing couple - foreigner.

III

What brings you to this place I want to escape?
Must we share another error?
We will keep our heads down in the rain,
ignore the street-corner sermons
- the last wheeze of revolution.

We're still on our knees, still soaked to the bone,
haunted by our lost children.
We have chosen this as home
and slip into our fate like Russian dolls
sinking inside ourselves, dropping through folds.

Mairtín Crawford

Mairtín Crawford was born in Belfast. He studied English Literature at Queen's University, Belfast. He co-edited *Gown Literary Supplement* and *The Big Spoon* in the 1980s and 1990s respectively and was literary editor of *Fortnight* magazine. In addition he taught creative writing in The Crescent Arts Centre (Belfast) and became Director of the Literary Festival there shortly before his death in January 2004. The poet's posthumous collection is *Mairtín Crawford: The Selected Poems* (Lagan Press, 2005).

Three locations are linked and recurrent in this poetry: Belfast, New York and outer space. 'St Patrick's Cross', for instance, by evoking the angst ridden life and smithereens style of the poet Padraic Fiacc, bridges the worlds of Belfast squats and New York's Hell's Kitchen. The remote, lonely and humanly challenging world of the astronaut who inhabits deep space - a place full of "fragments of aeons" and the "detritus" of "years of explosions and fission" - links, in turn, with the New York of Edward Hopper and Belfast. While the full range of the poetry makes use of traditional or inherited forms such as the sonnet, the sestina or couplet, there are forays into more "free-form" or experimental shapes; 'Backfire', for instance, begins and ends in the middle of violence, a still-born poem started and abandoned in mid-sentence. The shaky underbelly of Belfast (post the 1990s' ceasefires) and New York (post September 11th) emerge in poems like 'Afterwards' and 'Under the Bridge' respectively; along with other poems in Crawford's oeuvre these reveal a poet who has sensitively registered the inner life of contemporary cities and witnessed their fragility and veneer of civilisation. In a new millennium where space exploration is rapidly becoming frozen history the space poems attempt to keep alive its excitement and reality as a first love - an ongoing story involving courage, individuals, dreams, loves and desires. The space poems are, in short, a way of refracting light on earth.

Untitled Sonnet

What are we looking for all these years?
It can't be far from us though seasons change
light's sensuous quality and our perceptions
alter irrevocably. Like Autumn sunlight
its colder glance reminds us that there's
more to life than summers of indolent repose.
What we have we cannot help but lose.
None of it can go on forever.

But behind Winter there's always Spring.
You can't go on in silence imagining
the pure idea of silence. Look out
your window. The trees are waving in
unison because the dead are returning
to us, reborn, in new, perfect forms.

Going Away

We are always taking leave of each other.
There is somewhere else to go, another
friend to see, a bus to catch. It's a way
of unlearning love, to forget that the day
has just happened, running away from
something we can't control, the sum
total of despair written on our faces
the guilt that sends us to other places.

What do we leave behind then? A stain
on the sheets? More likely it is the pain
of knowing you are gone, the emptiness
of attics hung with nothing, the less
easy denial of loss that looms,
the silences of newly-painted rooms.

Saint Patrick's Cross

The character you describe in your
    unwritten
novels of the forties set
    in Hell's Kitchen
were just like you.
    They wanted to kill.
Life and Belfast -
    you returned to hell -
exploded and the wee girls cried.
Verse and moral companions were all
    you wanted.

The black and innocent half
    dead memories of
your own holy communion are soaked in
    blood now.
The passing of time is a simple
    ceremony
that ends in a state of
    entropy
in your Eglantine Avenue squat.

Pious! Ha! The Pope should
    visit you.
He'd learn something about morality and
    shit. Decay.
Difference between wrong and wrong.
    It's right
to kill. It's right to kill the night.

The plague of arguments and bad reviews
    didn't kill you.
The warmth you take from the guts of
    whiskey
belies the cold disquiet in the fiction
    we believe is a soul.

Backfire

I'd riddled the entire back wall,
cut it to bits, and then I'd ran
up the stairs and down the hall
the black taxi and the can
of worms I'd left unopened,
as an alibi. There was no trace
of the driver, who'd been subpoenaed
and I was sure I was no place.
It was bound to backfire -
the gun jammed and 'you'
were close behind me,
calling me a liar.
Perhaps the fiction's true,
though, as I

Afterwards

Outside the day is an explosion.
You are a collection of nudity
in someone else's poem,
with a face all angles of mistrust.
Later you ask me where the kettle is
and I am saying: 'I don't know
where the kettle is', trying to step
between the perfect riot
of cat and vengeful starlings
and the pile of books you have
erected as a barricade. In my defence
I plead ignorance and alien landmarks,
repeating, 'I don't know where the kettle
is, I don't know where I am.'

Under the Bridge

This is not the end - not nearly.
Remember, when you have your
story ready, tell them about the
Hudson, the grey water that turns
to light, the illicit naked waves,
the fairytale floating beyond.
The small details on the edge
and at the bottom of the bridge.
By looking down you create
a difference, the day's remnants
making their own importance:
the half-eaten souvlaki
squashed under the wheels of
a taxi, the stare of a hungry
bum, the spacemen in the village
and the image of your cigarette
lighter hanging on the precipice
of this girl's bed like a skyscraper.

Chop Suey
Edward Hopper, 1951

It's the eyes: how they are drawn
away from her friend to look out
at you, the dreamer, the one standing
still, beyond the frame and the border
of an era. The words written there
could be the name desire and the awful
perfection of an art that says she belongs
to yesterday, to no-one in particular.

Challenger

How high did you go, Christa, before
you knew you were starting to fall?
Were you thinking of some dead star
in Betelgeuse, of gamma rays, of life out there?
A hero's homecoming awaited you.
You were Amelia Earhart to us.
You challenged us all.

We still find pieces of you
washed up on the shore.
They tell us we should not look for you.
But no cover up can cover up this -
I love you, Christa, for all I'm worth.
Send me into space. Leave me there.
And who's to say those voices on the Internet
are not yours, or mine, or theirs?

Baikonur

For honour and promotion we built her.
A mining town that didn't exist. Two hundred
miles south of Kazakhstan. Baikonur. Nowhere.
Our Cosmodrome. We've launched hundreds
from here. Some you don't even know about yet.

Rockets. Spaceships. Proton. Soyuz. Gagarin.
Pride, yes - we won it from the skies and beyond.
Wild horses and camels roam our vast ranges.
We have a child. Her name is Zarya. She will live.

Life on Mars

If you looked through the world's most powerful telescope,
one like the Hubble, that can see as far away as Pluto and
even thousands of light years beyond that
what you might see are the fragments of aeons
        drifting away into dust,
the detritus of billions of years of explosions and fission.

If you were to cast your eye back over the centuries -
remembering millennia are a purely human notion -
would you see things run backwards and empires
        build themselves
up again? What way would time travel?

If you were to ask me if there was life on Mars
        I'd point to Mariner, Voyager,
and NASA experiments including spouting
        glowing ammonia into a vacuum chamber
trying to build the ultimate thruster to take us there.

Then I'd recite the names of the oceans, hills and valleys
        of Mars:
Ortygia, Moab, Oxus, Arabia, Cerberus, Memnonia, Hellas,
Electris, Cyclopia, Amazonis, Thoth, Utopia, Elysium.

Paula Cunningham

Paula Cunningham was born in Omagh, County Tyrone, in 1963. She studied Dentistry at Queen's University, Belfast. She has written a monologue for theatre, *The Silver Wake* (performed by Tinderbox in Belfast in 2000), co-written a radio play, *Kin* (broadcast on BBC Radio 4, 2002) and a new short story is included in the *Faber Book of Best New Irish Short Stories, 2004-5* (Faber, 2005). A short collection of her poetry was published as *A Dog Called Chance* (Smith/Doorstop Books, 1999) and selections of poems have been included in *Breaking the Skin: 21st Century Irish Writing: New Poetry* (Black Mountain Press, 2002), *New Soundings* (Blackstaff Press, 2003) and *New Irish Poets* (Bloodaxe Books, 2004).

In *A Dog Called Chance* the title sequence of poems explore the aftermath of the Omagh bomb of August 1998. The fixity and rigidity of politics in the North contrasts with poetry itself which, in 'Hats' for instance, is characterised by flexibility and experimentation - the "trying out" of voices and headgear. A recurrent fascination with human relationships lies at the centre of this poetry; it uses both telling detail and a flexible voice to chart the varieties, evolution, genetics and individualism of the relationships it describes. It is a rich, varied poetry too: there is the conversational irony and parody of Louis MacNeice in 'Too Dear'; the eroticism of 'Aubade'; the rueful hindsight which chart love's inevitable cooling ardour over time in 'At first our letters'; the witty balance of scepticism and faith in 'Cats - A Retrospective' and of the real and surreal in 'Seeing Things', the powerful pull of the subjective in 'Losing the keys' which is balanced by the terrifying tug of genetics and inheritance in 'Driving North'. If the public sphere interpenetrates or shadows the private there remains a sense that humour, irony and poetry itself offer ways of self-protection or self-awareness as well as ways of seeing the freedoms still available to us.

Hats

This year I tried on voices just like hats.

Whore hat
Bored hat
Life's a fucking chore hat
Tore hat
Sore hat
Never bloody score hat
Can't take any more hat
Roar hat
Soon be thirty-four hat.

I was running out of fabric

But then I found a blessed hat
Poetry obsessed hat
Need a bloody rest hat
Got to go out west hat
Realised that politics are best avoided
Put on my Sunday best hat
Soon got bored with that.

Tried on my dead serious issues hat
My rhyme all the time hat
My why can't I write like Paula Meehan hat
My fek it have a drink and write like Brendan Behan hat.

This year I tried on voices just like hats
The weather changed
The cease-fires came
And screaming like a banshee
My severed tongue grew back.

My father wore a hat when I was little
we lived in Omagh O-M-A-G-Haitch or -Aitch
depending on belief.

He was a travelling salesman for ice-cream;
a Dublin firm Hughes Brothers or H.B.
he was their Northern Ireland diplomat.

He knew his clients well - a studied discipline,
some would not buy HB ice-cream on principle.
My father'd done his homework;
to some he'd sell Haitch
B, to others Aitch B.

One day in Derry/Londonderry my father's car was hijacked.
The men wore hats pulled down with holes for eyes and mouth.
They held a gun, they nudged his hat.
They asked my father where we lived
and ordered him to spell it.

This year I tried on voices just like hats.

Too Dear

You said you'd phone me soon
I never thought to question you

Call me peak rate or never call

I said I'd trade a kiss for flowers
You said you'd do without

Call me peak rate or never call

At night you made my walls rebound
By day you could not spare a pound

Call me peak rate or never call

You took to calling once a week
On Sundays after six

Call me peak rate or never call

I realised the strings were false
I took my scissors from their box

Call me peak rate or never call

I cut the ties that did not bind
My dear, I was too dear for you

Call me peak rate or never call

Aubade

Bring the muse into the kitchen
            - Walt Whitman

A man is squeezing oranges in my kitchen.
I am down the corridor in bed
and he is squeezing oranges
in my kitchen.
From where I lie
I cannot see
the man
but I've deduced
that he
is squeezing oranges.

There is something tremendously erotic
about a man
squeezing oranges.
What is erotic is the sound.
This man

has found my orange squeezer
without my prompting.
He does not know I know
he's squeezing oranges.

Lying here, listening
to the sound of a man
secretly squeezing oranges
at 1.09 of a Sunday afternoon,
I am struck by the fact
That I've never heard any sound
quite so erotic
as the sound of a man
squeezing oranges.

At first our letters

always crossed
(we couldn't wait)
they weighed in heavy

over airmail
rate, bulging
with the future tense.

I fancied them as birds
stilling their wings
to touch or kiss

mid-flight, larks maybe
sparking the driest air
twenty, forty thousand feet

above sea-level;
unseasoned migrants
never settling into

a synchronous
simple harmonic.
All those songs of nesting

building together,
the location we couldn't ever
agree on, both of us

wanting it both ways,
native and exotic,
twigs, feathers

ferns in our mouths.
Where do we go from here?
your last letter

burned on my desk
for days - a thin affair.
I hesitate, a feather

in my throat.
Weeks pass;
I still can't lift the pen

to shift the tense,
and every night
I choke.

Cats - A Retrospective

I believe to have one dog is better than a hundred thousand cats
I believe whatever anybody older than me says
except my older sisters who know nothing
and our neighbours, the McCaugheys, who have far too many cats.

I believe what Mum and Dad, my teachers and the priests tell me is right
and that, believing them, I'll be right too.
I believe there's a right way of doing things,
I believe in the essential beauty of the thing done right

and in always, always doing the right thing.
I believe that any job worth doing is worth doing well
I believe that God's a Catholic, that he's everywhere
I believe it will be twenty years before I hear the thing

about the many ways to skin a cat and I believe
that even then I'll wonder which one's right.

Mother's Pride

Handy with a knife,
his preferred medium
was Mother's Pride plain toast.
This is the way the nuns

eat - soldiers;
this is the Protestant
half. Here's Omagh, Belfast,
Enniskillen, Dublin, Donegal

with Errigal hastily moulded
from Clew Bay, a crumb
for an island for every day

of the year, and Cork,

where John Mac lives.
Lough Erne's two narrow slits;
Lough Neagh his index
finger poked right through.

A final flourish, grinning,
his *pièce de résistance*
was the border,
which my frowning mother

quickly buttered over,
stabbing the bread
and drawing
the knife out clean.

Seeing Things

At the Winter Park ski-holiday reunion
who swans in only Stevie
whose legs don't take him far
- he'd been tinkering under a car
when the bomb went off.

Answer: the skin.
It's trivia night
and we're in with a chance.
All the other tables are offering liver.
What is the largest organ in the body?

In Winter Park we're triple-wrapped
in thermals
but he's shirtless:
a sophisticated instrument
of thermo-regulation.

Homeostasis: the body
is a furnace.
The sweat-glands
and erector pili muscles
co-operate to keep the body cool.

The hypothalmus
is conductor of the body's
secret business;
but skin grafts don't have glands
and scars are bald.

Anyway Stevie has walked
the twenty yards from his special car
and he's wrecked
and his stumps are sore
and we get tore in to the drink

and we all get legless
and everyone in the Welly Bar
(we're only here for the ramps
and we've jumped the queue)
is legless and Stevie has taken his off

all smooth American tan
with the socks and the cool shoes on
and we laugh out loud
at the pretty woman
on stilts who almost

jumps out of her skin
and the plastered people
who swear
they're seein' things
and we know they are.

Because

they do not usually borrow
your underwear and

there is nothing in the woman
that compares to the silk

of scalp over bone when the hair
leaves. This and the miracle

of stubble. There is
no equivalent either to returning

after a long day at the office, a day
sufficient to make you forget

the man who stayed,
and finding the loo seat

up. The way their water
falls, louder & unmuffled,

akin sometimes to music
or children's laughter,

and the way they stand, their eyes
already far-off trancers

following the band. The household bill
for toilet roll decreases; feminine

hygiene costs are also down. Mostly
they earn more anyway, have better

motors & prefer to drive, improving
fuel economy. Sperm is also

a consideration. The way a ball
will fall quite unabashed

from their shorts
while the small amphibian

sleeps in its scratchy nest.
The way you always get

to read them first,
and y-fronts

on the washing line
the only flags

that ever
make you smile.

Losing the Keys

Losing the keys I'm at a loss again;
though I lock myself out in all weathers
it would appear I specialise in grey skies, rain.

Losing the keys or dreading losing them
it's all the same, the art of losing being
well established in my head,

I set my mind on damage limitation, spares
buried in flowerbeds, lodged with friends; I don
bright Gortex, carry an umbrella like a prayer.

But worse than being stranded on your own
doorstep in rain is getting in, no sweat, let's say
a sunny day, chubbing the door, putting on

the chain, losing the keys inside the house,
sitting indoors outside yourself again.

Driving North

Returning late in rain from Connemara,
each time we pass a 'Welcome to our County'
I slow and sound the horn, a single toot,

Galway, *toot*, Mayo, *toot*, Sligo…
and I'm explaining 'My first real boyfriend,
Davy, did this twenty years ago.'

And when approaching sleep you call me sweetie
I know your friend, your ex, still calls you that;
and later when you flex and click your knuckles

you will tell me of a lover, way back,
who'd twist and stretch so ardently
that every single vertebra would crack.

And when you make me scratch your back
it's childhood and your daddy; the wheaten
bread each Saturday's my ma; that thing

when I touch the back of your hand
with the back of a hot coffee spoon's a man
I loved abysmally and that man's granddad.

And this is how it is:
angels and ogres jostle at our shoulders
anxious for their chance to vanquish time;

and these fleeting appearances, *toot*, brief visitations
that warm and make us smile
keep all of our losses, even our dead, alive.

Moyra Donaldson

Moyra Donaldson was born in Newtownards in 1956. She studied English Literature and Language at Queen's University, Belfast. A poetry pamphlet, *Kissing Ghosts* (Lapwing Press, 1995) and screenplay *'h'* (filmed in 1996) appeared before the publication of two poetry collections, *Snakeskin Stilettos* (Lagan Press, 1998) and *Beneath the Ice* (Lagan Press, 2001). She currently lives between Bangor and Newtownards.

Central to these poetry collections are an exploration of both the personal (family, parents, daughters, love, adultery) and the public (the 'North' and its religious and political legacies and inherited expectations of duty and morality); the interrelationships between these two terrains provide tensions, which lie at the core of many poems. A public inheritance (guilt from religion or male/ paternal moralities) often wages war with individual desire or contemporary female sexuality; the poetry seeks to marry lyrical and dramatic modes to explore this tension, to find its own map or way home. Fairytale, riddle and the short story (as well as the language and imagery of mythology and Christianity) are inextricably woven through the fabric of many poems. The poetry seeks a myth or spirituality adequate to carrying both the promises and failings of the actual as well as the imagined world of the poems. Location and the North of Ireland, while virtually absent, are often present by implication in the poems; locale, however, does not operate so much as a physical landscape but, rather, as inner state or terrain, often grasped as a negative space and resisted before becoming grist for imaginative reclamation or the projection of possibilities. Poems like 'Exile' pit poetry and paganism against the lack of transcendence in institutional Protestantism; 'I Do Not' frustrates both Catholic or poetic traditions of the confessional and resists the cliché of Protestant guilt. These poems bear witness to a poet who is determined, like the artist Cesar Manrique, to find 'spaces' or air-bubbles on a volcanic island - places where it is possible to work through the lack of "magic" in religion or "transcendence" in politics and still find "beauty in paucity, metamorphosis in fire".

Exile

What ground is mine
if I would govern myself?
Where is my country
if neither bogs nor gantries
speak of me?
Where can I stand
if I am not one thing,
or the other?

My grandfather knew where he stood.
Ancestors planted his feet
in fertile soil, green futures were
named in his name, possessed.
He preached their flinty faith
in mission tents, visions of eternal life
on soft Ulster evenings,

but there was no redemption.
Not in the land, or through the Blood.
Not in the hard lessons of duty, obedience,
with which he marked his children.

He is stripped of virtue,
his legacy a stone
of no magic, no transcendence.
No children ever turn to swans,
Wafer remains wafer on the tongue,
and flesh is always flesh.

My two white birds will bring me
water from the mountains,
beakfuls of sweet sips.
I will grow a new tongue,
paint my body with circles
and symbols of strength, mark myself
as one who belongs in the desert.

Snakeskin Stilettos

Eight years old, you understand
these shoes are different.
Not for nothing
has your mother wrapped them in paper,
shut them into their box, set them
at the very back of the wardrobe.
Forbidden.

You imagine them -
on their own in the dark,
hissing softly.
Biding their time.

Sneak in, creak open the door,
lift the lid and let them out,
untissue the fear.
Run your fingers
against the fissley scales,
press the fangs of heels
into your palm.
Something
you've never felt before.
These shoes are live and dangerous.

Infidelities

After he'd gone,
she found money in the sheets,
fallen when he pulled his trousers off.
Gathering the coins into a small pile
she set them on the window ledge.
They sat, gathering dust, guilt,
until one day her husband
scooped them into his pocket.
Small change for a call
he couldn't make from the house.

Driving Back Alone from Mayo

No need for signposts
in a country crisscrossed
with trails of other journeys,
winter sun at my back
pushing me east.
I bless each familiar thing
and set my mind on constancy,
telling myself stories we could become,
re-inventing our history.
I was faithful, content,
love made you articulate.
The fiction of what should have been
is a map unfolding, a way home.

Lethe

My poor mother,
for your birthday you get another 'little episode',
another transient ischaemic attack,
during which you walk into a door jamb.
Your face is bruised, as if you'd been punched
hard and when I ask if it hurts, you say
'I don't think so.' You are even more lost.
If only misery could be wiped away like memory,
like chalk marks from a board, lessons over.

My poor mother,
your bones are light as the memory of bones,
and your flesh is melted to a dream of flesh.
My heart is broken by your lightness,
by your terrible absence, as you rest
what is left against my shoulder.
I cannot help you: there is no comfort,
and this is too cruel
no matter what our sins have been.

My poor mother,
your children are un-able, for even now
your need is not greater than ours
and we have never known how.
Forgive us our trespasses
as we have forgiven your trespasses
against us. Deliver us
from this evil. Where is the river,
the beautiful, the beautiful, the river?

Anecdotal Words

I

She works nightshift, security, watching
the monitors, walls of glass, fragments
of city centre streets, moments of lives.
She sees all kinds of things pass by, tight knots
of drama, quick fucks in doorways, fights, tears
in the rain, drunks pissing against the wind.
Sometimes she dreams up histories, allows
these anecdotal thoughts to swell, become
stories for strangers moving through the dark -
like these two, faces lost in static snow.
Bereft of meaning or context, she gives
them hopelessness, illicit love, and ice,
a monster trapped inside a glacier,
a virus underneath the permafrost.

II

Belfast Sunday is no place for late night might-be lovers:
cold streets and closed doors, nowhere to go.
A security camera records their uncertainty,
him and her in a black and white loop, a B-movie,
grainy from re-running. She's shivering
and he leans against a stone façade, holds her
as the winter wind winds her coat around them.

He's offering anecdotal evidence of warmth,
and though his words have rhythm and scansion
she knows they prove nothing, he will always be
nine-tenths hidden. Her words are a frozen weir
where a woman floats, dreaming beneath the ice.
His kisses will not warm her, nothing will melt -
there will never be anything between them but regret.

Applying Fuzzy Logic

To find your own niche in love's conceptual anarchy
forget Aristotle and his either/or logic -
go for fuzzification instead: the cocaine of science.

Enter your lover's linguistic variables, his if-then rules,
his vagueness, paradoxes and information granulation
into the Kosko Fuzzy Approximation Theorem.
Make use of the machinery

for dealing with imprecision and partial truth.
The outcome will define where love stands for you
on the continuum between completely true and completely false.

This allows you a closer rapport with reality,
and can substantially increase your power.

Ulster Says No

Having grown up with so many given negatives
I am always and constitutionally inclined to say yes
yes let's have another drink
yes go on ahead
yes of course you can
yes I'll try that
yes why not?
yes have some of mine
even when it might be more prudent to decline.

Cesar Manrique

You used an island
for your canvas,
flourished in a desert home
of unremitting hardness
by finding out hollows,
spaces where air held back
molten rock, created
a place to live and grow
like lichen, a new beginning.
You tempted the wind with toys,
listened to the music
that stone offered to your ear,
deep magic of caves,
beauty in paucity,
metamorphosis in fire.

My small daughter christens you
our man Reeki
catching my feeling
that you and I
are on the same side.

I Do Not

I do not confess to anything - so when I speak
of the small dark spidery creature
skittling across the periphery of my vision -
it proves nothing.
Meaning is just an accident,
soon mopped up - those letters
were written by someone else,
and that suitcase under the bed
does not contain my heart.

I do not regret anything - so when the black dog
digs up the bones I have buried
beneath the brambles, deep in the wild woods -
I am not worried.
I have allowed no prophets
to enter my house, so bones can not
stand up, grow flesh and walk.
They cast no shadows
and I have nothing to look in the face.

I do not promise anything - so when I lie
down with you, close as a child,
intimate as a lover, tender as a mother -
it means nothing.
Love is just a trick of the light,
a misunderstanding.
No matter who you think I am,
when it matters most,
I will not be who you want.

Dan Eggs

Dan Eggs is a singer, poet and performance artist. His albums include *More Songs About Everyday Objects (1), More Songs About Everyday Objects (2), Esoteric Epigrams, Seascapes and Spoken Word*. His debut volume of poems and songs was entitled *Dan Eggs' Big 99* (Lagan Press, 2003).

In Dan Eggs' poetry everyday and household objects rub shoulders with the bizarre and surreal. The poetry is reminiscent of the apparent nonsense poems of Spike Milligan; poems often attempt, humorously, to "tell how the laundry basket squeaked" (Katherine Mansfield's phrase). Many poems have close links with popular songs and popular culture (ballads, doggerel and nonsense verse) and, consequently, masculine internal rhyme is a key motor. The satirical edge in the verse is also apparent in poems which attempt to debunk human pretension or hypocrisy and to affirm human or humorous values. In direct epigrams, epitaphs, parodies, short first person statements (which sometimes pose as naïve) or through an oblique ventriloquism, the poems give 'apparently ordinary' people or objects an extraordinary voice or distance from which it is possible to satirise our foibles and to affirm a more human ideal. This is poetry that veers between fearlessly direct statement which uncovers both slight and significant truths (that adults know but only children speak of) and indirect ventriloquism (that bursts the balloons of our pretensions and presumptions of knowing anything at all).

In Belfast

In Belfast, the future we see through the past, parallel
talks could collapse, sea swell - sky overcast, but
sunny spell laughs are forecast, where's the hotel's
what is asked, end-of-school bell - out of class, the
moment is all that can last, in Belfast, in Belfast, in
Belfast, in Belfast.

Five Short Poems

When I Die

When I die, eat a fry and remember me as Davy, or
cook a spud, in the mud and dance upon my gravy.

Clean Yourself, Mate

Shadows in the night move unseen, heartache owl, time
you preened.

Oh, My Name Is Dan Eggs

Oh, my name is Dan Eggs, I've got long hairy legs,
And I like to relax in my crimplene slacks.

The End of Childhood

They gave me a pen and they told me to write.

Parody

If a swordfish was rammed up your arse (sideways),
would you be comfortable? Of course you wouldn't.

Seagulls

I know it is Sunday, because there isn't any cars, and
there's lots of empty packets, outside the hot food bars.
I'm a seagull in the morning, a seagull in the night,
please help me in my lifestyle of greedy needy plight.
The twenty-four hour shift beneath the yellow neon
lights, I hover in the salt air where drunken sailors fight.
And after they get back to ship, breaking bottles on the
way, I thank my seagull saviour at the dawning of the
day.

Astronaut's Wife's Heartache

You have left this planet, the pillow is wet with my
tears, I cry myself to sleep, you are a clot in my blood,
a knot in my brain, I'll probably never see you again.
Together, Cape Canaveral, watching the sea, my
mother, grandmother, brother and me.

Spin Dryer and Washing Machine

The spin dryer's moved in with the washing machine,
they're living together, you know what I mean, I believe the spin dryer's
the clothes bin's mum, he came out of her rotating aerated drum,
she takes the day off when the weather's fine, then he does a line
with the clothes line, they live in an outhouse without any fuss, are
these household appliances quite like us? (The washing machine once
spilt his load because he was in fast coloureds mode).

Sunday Morning

The cow in the field chews the grass, she never thinks about going to Mass, the little bird sitting high on the birch, he and his friends don't think about church, the wasps in the dustbin devouring the apple, what do they know about going to chapel, the elderly lady sits in her pew, while her young son watches Kung Fu.

Mop and Mop Bucket

'We'll stick together - things won't go amiss, we'll give a lasting dependable service, it doesn't pay to do that home help hassle, stay with me - rest in my vessel, we're best friends - we get along fine, complete with our ergonomic handle design, I therefore take thee to be my lawful wedded mop bucket, I will stand in you, I mean by you, I will not fade, chip, peel, dent, warp, leak, crack or rust, honest, promise, I will not splash, spill or slop. I will be your Flash-filled matrimonial mop', that's what I heard happening in the kitchen, the mop and the mop bucket didn't know I was listening, it's strange what goes on, on a roll of linoleum, when you eavesdrop on objects without them knowing.

Three Numbers

I'd like to give you three numbers. The first is my national insurance number... WM 735797A.
Second is my bank account number, 92778066,
and the third one is my Pin number, No, hang on, I better not give you that one.

Windmill

When fishies in the sea are all swimming free, I'll see
you in the land across the water, when Trident
submarines are windmill machines, I'll see you in the
land across the water, and you want to go, and I want to
stay, and long-distance love will sometimes fade away.
When BNFL can no longer sell, I'll see you in the
land across the water, when everything's agreed and
they shut Sellafield, I'll see you in the land across the water and when
we're together, we talk about the weather, be careful on your way,
the sea is rough today.

Boat

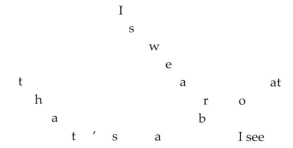

Leontia Flynn

Leontia Flynn was born in Belfast in 1974. She was awarded a major Eric Gregory Award in 2001; her first volume of poems was entitled *These Days* (Jonathan Cape, 2004).

Leontia Flynn writes with both wry bemusement and tenderness about love, everyday events, the North of Ireland and the literary tradition. The poems often enact delicate, slight, shifts in our consciousness via the accumulated use of tellingly suggestive, small details so that a whole submerged landscape or key moment yields its significance. A cigarette burn hole in a woollen jumper signifies the dying spark of one private revolution with a job in the civil service; "billowing" Styrofoam balls from a delivery van amount to an epiphany like Tarkovsky's snow; one school book stands in for a whole teenage summer. The poems also deploy cadence and subtle (often wistful) harmonies, conversational and complex syntax, precise, concentrated images (which double as symbols), renovated clichés and suggestive ambiguities; the result is that poems leave a wealth of implication or wonder in their wake. As in Paul Muldoon's view of Robert Frost (a poet Flynn transposes into an urban Scotland) - underneath the apparent simplicity all kinds of complicated things are happening. Some poems explore standard themes - memories of childhood, the way perception or love alters with time, the nature of language itself - but in such a way that we are surprised into new meanings and knowledge or shocked into seeing what we already know precisely redefined in words. The "Without Me" sequence of poems reveals a capacity to reflect on the same subject - literal loss, but retention in the memory - in many different images. In this poetry knowledge of the literary or film traditions is often worn lightly but deployed to serious, subversive or playful effect. The result is a wealth of short lyrics that are terse, tender, pithy, granular - and very much alive.

Come Live with Me

Come live with me and be my mate
and all the fittings and the fixtures of the flat
will burst with joy -
                    this flowered ottoman, this tallboy.
I'll leave a water-ring around your heart.
In the mildewed kitchenette of afternoon
T.V., my cup of coffee
overfloweth. *Neighbours. Ironside.*
Whatever Happened to Baby Jane?
- that well-known scene in which, as you explain, the
    feral heel
Of Bette Davis meets Ms Crawford's head - head on -
    for real ! for real !

For Stuart, who Accidentally Obtained a Job in the Civil Service

I have it in my diary as May the 6th
and a beautiful evening. We walk in silence
back to my house. There are condolences;
sitting round as though we are at a wake,
somebody mentions Kafka.

You explain about your mother.
For now, I tell you, just for now…
the evening light and a spark, fallen
from your cigarette butt onto the woolly jumper
over your truculent heart, quietly dying.

Games

They have taken Kevin off the machine for Christmas.
The lights are on -
but his mouth keeps working, over and over:
Ouzo. Sambuca. Jägermeister.
We hold his free hand like the string of a kite.

Later that night, it's a double shot in the dark:
retracing our steps from A to A
and the flat where we learned, strategically, to down a
    bridge
        too far -
We move beyond the pint of no return.

Without Me

Without me and without you, what's the point
of the fact that you fried onions like you were
    harpooning shrimp
in a wok found in a skip near a flat on Wellesley?
And what's the point of the three-and-a-half years spent
- like fifteen minutes at a bus-stop - if as casually
as my glib wave, when something moves from my hand,
or the road receding in the driver's mirror,
we are gone?
        Suddenly it's beyond me:
how I'm turning my thoughts to the bird or two in the
    bush
and to all the fish in the intervening sea.

Without Me

Once, in the hiatus of a difficult July,
down Eskra's lorryless roads from sweet fuck all,
we were flinging - such young sophisticates - like a giant
    frisbee
this plastic lid of an old rat-poison bin.

We were flinging it from you to me, me to you, you to
    me;
me-you, you-me, me-you, you back again.
And you would have sworn that its flat arc was a
    pendulum,
compassing Tyrone's prosy horizon.

And I would have sworn that our throw and catch had
    such momentum
that its rhythm might survive, somehow, without me.

What You Get

Two roads diverge in South Gyle Industrial Estate
and you would take the one less travelled by
if it were not, you think, possibly the cul-de-sac
where the snack vans park at night, or where the trucks
are moored, fed and watered, after their delivery
of precious things.
                One afternoon you watch
as a host of Styrofoam balls comes billowing through
and covers the close: a great Andrei Tarkovsky
slo-mo, and you're pleased with it -
its basic wage, take-what-you-get epiphany.

Bed Poem

bed, the word, is almost a child's
picture poem, a hieroglyph spelling itself:
the stroke of the b forming a bedpost on one side
and the stroke of the d the bedpost on the other.

Surely, at some stage - perhaps
down the black pits of winter mornings - everyone
has felt the urge to go Florence Nightingale:

                                                    just

forget this whole business of penetrating
and directing a day. Take to our lazy beds.
Let the days have their way with us.

Imagine the heavy comfort of curtains…
I would lay my ear to the mattress and test the weight
    of bed words:

    moony   goosefeather   incubus

against my tongue. I would listen to the deep
grinding harmonies of the bedsprings.

The Furthest Distances I've Travelled

Like many folk, when first I saddled a rucksack,
feeling its weight on my back -
the way my spine
curved under it like a meridian -

I thought: Yes. This is how
to live. On the beaten track, the sherpa pass, between
    Krakow

and Zagreb, or the Siberian white
cells of scattered airports,

it came clear as over a tannoy
that in restlessness, in anony
mity:
was some kind of destiny.

So whether it was the scare stories about Larium
- the threats of delerium
and baldness - that led me, not to a Western Union
wiring money with six words of Lithuanian,

but to this post office with a handful of bills
or a giro; and why, if I'm stuffing smalls
hastily into a holdhall, I am less likely
to be catching a Greyhound from Madison to
    Milwaukee

than to be doing some overdue laundry
is really beyond me.
However,
when, during routine evictions, I discover

alien pants, cinema stubs, the throwaway
comment - on a Post-it - or a tiny stowaway
pressed flower amid bottom drawers,
I know these are my souvenirs

and, from these crushed valentines, this unravelled
sports sock, that the furthest distances I've travelled
have been those between people. And what survives
of holidaying briefly in their lives.

These Days
for Catherine Donnelly

These days, it seems, I am winding my clock an hour
    forward
with every second weekend, and the leaves on my Marc
    Chagall calendar
flip as though they are caught in some covert draught.
These days I haven't time for people on television or
    aeroplanes
who say 'momentarily' meaning 'in just one moment'.

These days - these days which are fairly unremarkable -
light falls, outside of my window, on the red brick planes
where the trees are coming into leaf. These are the days
of correcting the grammar on library-desk graffiti,
the cheap, unmistakeable thrill of breaking a copyright
    law.

But these days, like Cleopatra's Antony, I fancy bestriding
    the ocean;
these days I am serious. These days I'm bowled over
hearing myself say *ten years ago this… ten years ago
    such-and-such*
like the man left standing, his house falling wall by wall,
in that black-and-white flick blurring headlong into
    colour.

Casablanca, backwards

Rick (to Ilse): Who are you really and what were you before?
What did you do and what did you think?

A plane is taking off in a bank of fog.
It leaves the grainy sky, the mapped Moroccan sand.
It is four months since I've seen you. In my hand
the video's controls point in the air.
"Who were we really and what were we before?"
These things are turning over in my mind

as the plane starts banking down. It comes to land
on a grainy fog bank on a concrete plane.
Casablanca backwards; in this version
Rick Blaine sticks his neck out - really - for no one.
As time does not go by. As history gives way to love -
all the rain of Morocco is raining back to the source!
the rain-soaked note resolving into words.
One tear streams back up Ingrid Bergman's face.

Sam Gardiner

Sam Gardiner was born in Portadown, County Armagh, in 1936. He has lived in London and Lincolnshire for the past thirty years. Apart from years compiling and editing the *Poet's Yearbook* and occasional bouts of journalism and reviewing, his working life has been spent in architecture. His first volume of poems was entitled *Protestant Windows* (Lagan Press, 2000). He has also written *The Picture Never Taken* (Smith/Doorstep Books, 2004).

In Sam Gardiner's poetry the North of Ireland is placed under a microscope and displaced through binoculars. The poet's Ulster childhood, parents and inherited baggage (ancestral, religious and political) are depicted and examined in detail by an insider and subjected to wry humour and humane study, to understatement and irony, to the scepticism and sympathy of a poet who has made comparisons and lived elsewhere. Protestantism emerges from the poems as utterly but excessively principled. In fact, the gaps and tensions between the North's inherited, religious (in)sensitivities and the secular world where religion is peripheral offer the poet rich scope for ambiguity, balanced irony or Swiftian satire. The poetry, often iconoclastic in relation to institutional belief, is frequently tender in affirming the tenacity of the individuals, recording trials of faith and despair or in charting the vicissitudes of love. The love poems are very fine. Accessible and engaged, the deceptive simplicity of the poetry's language should obscure neither the dexterity nor architecture of the complex verse forms used nor the multi-vocal dialogues they open up. The poet's guises are legion: teacher, doctor, twelve year old, son, lover, singer, and philosopher. The poetry, however, is also conscious of the limits and strengths of language itself; the deadpan humour of 'No Title', 'Sanity Tablets' or 'Colorado Desert Night' (not included in this anthology) manage to balance both anti-transcendental and mysterious views of the world in two thinks at one time. This is a poetry that loves paradox, double vision and "infinite possibilities"; it can ask in one and the same breath - "Who am I? Who else am I/not?" While drawing strength from English poets such as Thomas Hardy and Philip Larkin the poetry is in thrall to neither the traditions nor the poets which it evokes in its own benevolent scepticism.

Not at Home

On belonging and being tired of it,
of having to stay and change the world
or stay the world and change. I broke
away to the time-out of crowds.

Twelve months in London and I began
commuting by way of Trafalgar Square
to visit my father's pigeons, the ones
he waited for on a distant hillside.

Eyes peeled skywards for specks
barely moving above blue trees,
loaded shotgun against the fence
for pigeon-fancying peregrines

he waited long weekends for pigeons
who stayed away instead of homing in
on that stifling, hawk-eyed pigeon loft
in an endless drift of open fields.

Who said, 'This world is not our home'?
I forget, but he was right; as you are
when you leave a message complaining
that I'm never at home. I never was.

I Never Thanked You For

: giving me life, giving me death;
the dog and gun days;
the time you spent making box-kites
that got away;
the mushrooming before breakfast;

showing me the ropes
for hauling bales of linen and binding corn;
the bible-beltings
and the wrongs that were good for me
(I miss them);

the games of draughts you lost on purpose,
and the fights you won
in Sunday kitchens full of loud,
blue-chinned, argumentative uncles;
the big hand at school prizegivings

and for being twice the man
that Colin Medlow's father was,
and Errol Furst's, and Charlie McCreedy's;
sparing the rod
when I paddled across the flooded quarry
in a waterlogged wardrobe;

no living daylights beaten out of me,
of course I did it again, am still doing it.
And I never thanked you for suddenly
dying
to show me how it's done.

RIP Mrs. Farquhar RIP

Mrs. Farquhar was a gnarled, irascible recluse
when I was 12, and no older twenty years later
when she was taken away, presumably to die. But
if you are still alive, Mrs. Farquhar, and reading this,
you will see that the lad you always knew would come
to a bad end is declining nicely.
No one knew your story, or needed to. Yesterday's
stories were like that, but today, today was different.

Alone in her two-storey family home, monkey-puzzle
at the front and five or six apple trees (Beauties of Bath,
delicious) round the back, Mrs. Farquhar spent her days
knitting socks for her war-dead sons. We sniggered
behind her back, never to her scarlet face
and knobbly walking stick. 'There will always be wars
and rumours of wars,' she would assert, shaking her stick
and clearly prepared to start one single-handed.

She spoke with awesome authority
on the Black Death and the Great Potato Famine,
having survived both, apparently.
And she remembered 1641 as if it were yesterday:
the massacre of Protestants on the bridge in Portadown.
Sluggish with the corpses of settlers
from Worcestershire, the river slowly twisted and turned
red. The sky flowed white and blue.

The Passed On were more real than the Still Here,
and when I raided her little orchard until she gave me
sixpence to pull the ripe apples and store them in trays
in her shed, she was saving bygones, not apples.
One of the new, everything goes, know-alls, I waved
(slightly) when the Queen drove past the end of the lane
and loitered not seen to be listening when de Valera
grieved from the back of a coal lorry in Union Street.
Mrs. Farquhar lived in other times, we told one another.

Until the killing started. Distant relatives, we assumed
they were relatives so distant she had written them off,
took her away and the house stood empty. Somehow,
Beauties of Bath lost their flavour.
RIP, Mrs. Farquhar, and congratulations - you were right.
But apologies if you are still with us, which I suspect
you are. In fact, the evidence is overwhelming.

Protestant Windows

They come at sunset peddling daylight, two
salesmen wearing glasses, through which they view
his shabby sliding sashes with disdain.
'Wood?' they suppose and feign
dismay. 'Yes, comes from trees,'
and he raises the drawbridge ten degrees,
a hurdle to reservists
but child's play to front-line evangelists
with news of paradise
on earth (at this address to be precise)
in whitest white PVC.
                    'Think of all
the blessings. And if economical
heavenly comfort isn't what you need,
think of Our Earth,' they plead,
and their plastic-rimmed, double, glazed eyes glow
with love for generations of window
salesmen as yet unborn. 'If I were you,
I'd save my CO_2
for atheists and papists. I doubt
they even know about
King Billy.' 'Who?' 'William III to you,
brought sliding sashes to
Britain, fetched in pure air and sanity.
Without him we'd still be
in the dark.'

'Sorry, we must go. It's late,'
they say, and beat a retreat to the gate,
and pause. Quick as a flash
he raises an effortlessly sliding sash
for a parting shot. 'Plastic heretics!'
he shouts. The window sticks.

He tugs, a sash-cord snaps, the window drops
on his head, where it stops.
Latimer and Ridley know how he feels
as bloodied, martyred for his faith, he reels
towards eternity,
where planets, the latest novelty,
are looking less and less
like being a success.

Good Dog
*In 1722, the rector of Drumcree, Dr. Tisdall, received his old
acquaintance, Dean Swift.*

Protestant dogs are loyal, too loyal
for those they are loyal to, and loveable,
but when attacked tend not to mince their words,
just the shanks of their critics. Guard-dogs,
guide-dogs and underdogs by nature,
they are distressed to have to bludgeon re-
publicans and sinners to death with their tails
when the democratic process fails.
Protestant dogs once roamed the British Isles
sniffing out incense, false ideals, idols,
sacramental sex complete with penance
and all the purgatorial nonsense
dished out by Rome. Now penned in Ulster, they roam
unnerved and only feel at home at home.

Protestant dogs, who enjoy a direct
line to God (they ring on Sundays, cheap rate),
weep for their priest-ridden neighbours, but some
people you just can't help - damnation suits them.
Protestant dogs, though menaced on one side
by a tagged rabble of Gaels, wild with greed,
and on the other by an avalanche
of backsliding Saxons, give not an inch
but march the streets in the rain, up and down,
playing silver flutes, rattling drums for crown
and country, out of step but not caring,
up and down in the rain, not surrendering.

A van parks in Portadown, Market Street,
packed with explosive. In the passenger seat
a Protestant dog, a golden retriever, completes
the ideal family as he waits. And waits.
'Good dog,' the policeman says, trying
the door handle in vain. Then comes the warning.

The bomb destroys a dozen shops. The dog
is blown to bits, vanishes in a red fog.
The RSPCA decline to comment.
The Kennel Club are unmoved, they resent
an ancient pedigree which reaches back
through Calvin and Wyclif to Noah's Ark.
Blown-up, talked down, Protestant dogs don't shrink;
they are too busy being not extinct.

No Title

There are things we need words for,
like enamel jug, buttercups, crusty loaf,

and things we don't, such as love,
subatomic particles, that shooting star,

and there are words we need things for, God,
for example, ghosts, the verse in the universe.

But nothing needs words for us,
no thing looks us up in books and thinks,

How interesting, I must look out for one.

Sanity Tablets

Ghosts? No problem. We've got pills for phantoms.
I find chlorpromazine (only 40p
for twenty) useful for treating symptoms
like yours. Side effects? Rare, but apathy,

impotence and death have been noted. Still,
I wouldn't worry; strength of dose depends
on whether your spooks are as quick to kill
as, for instance, imaginary friends.

You have principles? I see, Apparitions
debase religion, mock the spiritual?
OK. Let's have no more visions or Virgins
and you can forget angels on the steeple.
Take these pills: become one of the reasons
why ghosts no longer believe in people.

Principia Poetica

This is Lesson 3 of 12. Let us start
high on the left and step down line by line.
The page must be held at an angle, thus,
the top farther away, the bottom nearer
so that it points directly at the heart.
The poem will advance down the incline
towards you as you read, the added impetus
assisting progress towards and by the reader.

Come into the sun. Watch it move from left
to right - the sun, not the poem. Look round:
your shadow also moves left to right
and the pen's natural path is demonstrated.
Antipodean poets often felt
hemispherically challenged and, having found
they had to view life through their legs to write
like Europeans, upped and emigrated.

Poems are not built upwards from the ground
like summer-houses, hotels and pagodas.
They are heavily built, stage upon stage.
Words however are lighter than air
and have to be caught in flight and pulled down.
The story of upward writing as good as
proves the case. Go to the foot of the page;
write upwards, piling lines above each other.

Quiet! Now, note these inky smudges and scuffs
where, alas, you sullied the line below.
Scribes who wrote this way were finally demoted,
heavily fined, and berated by their wives
for coming home from work with ink-stained cuffs.
Poetically, downwards is the way to go. The next lesson,
Lesson 4, is devoted
to feet, and why they must march past in fives.

Singing Today

Comet with white nightdress flying,
the startling. That's the universe,
and so is this *Good Bird Guide*
I'm about to show to this woman
who is also the universe.
And today is the day. Not that yesterday
belongs to people and places
I regret and would rather forget,
though she is none of them
Can you hear the singing bird?

Nor that so little is worth remembering,
though she is most of it, and more
with each astounding sun.
Today's the day because the chances
of our meeting in the multi-storey
in one of those collisions not covered
by insurance, or of her
standing here this morning
by this open window on the garden
Can you hear the springbird singing?

Or of life on any star system
anywhere, are ten to the power
of 40,000 to one against,
which means that every time we kiss
- and each time is the first time ever
since nothing happens twice -
I win every lottery in the universe,
first prize, bingo, jackpot,
jillpot if you like, life, love, the lot.
Can you hear me singing, bird?

Thinking of You

I spent last night burning all your letters.
Today I stray from room to room and try
to remember your last address, and whether
I promised your faithful hamster would die

smashed against the walls, which incidentally
are magnolia now, magnolia all the way
because you loathed it. And environmentally
sound, undyed toilet rolls have had their day.

My trolley shrieks with rolls of every hue:
apricot, strawberry, peach. I like to think
that when, in your memory, I flush the loo,
gradually a warm, suggestive pink
will spread across the long, cold miles of sea,
and you will look at it, and think of me.

Alan Gillis

Alan Gillis was born in 1973 in Belfast. He studied Literature at Queen's University before working at the Seamus Heaney Centre for Poetry. He has co-edited, with Aaron Kelly, *Critical Ireland: New Essays on Literature and Culture* (Four Courts Press, 2001) and written a critical study entitled *Irish Poetry of the 1930s* (Oxford University Press, 2005). His first poetry collection is *Somebody, Somewhere* (Gallery Press, 2004).

This is a poetry which multi-tasks; it celebrates "the drunkenness of things being various" (Louis MacNeice) and the strangeness of language itself. The chilly Belfast of 'Cold Flow' is a confection of sensuous freight and marketing jargon with "colour-fleck cars and butterfly people sprinkling/their hundreds and thousands across the soft icing roads." Energetic sentences, dense imagery, clever rhythms and rhymes (deployed and withheld), compound words, coinages and carefully controlled syntax all swerve, shimmer and simmer in the melting pot. The contemporary world of trademarked products, advertisements, popular music, street slabber, nicknames, gaming machines, violence and drink-and-drugs parties all swim in the soup. Boundaries between the real, imagined and surreal life of a city like Belfast collapse and are reconfigured again. The city emerges as a place of connection and disconnection, violence and imagination, breakdown and repair, memory and fragmentation. The impression left by the poetry is that of a richly layered fruitcake or a multi-track with an inbuilt resistance to (or anticipation of) reductive critique or paraphrase. The close, precise observation of minute detail, selective ear for different types of telling "slabber" and apparently meandering narratives are poetic features shared with Ciaran Carson's *Belfast Confetti*. The poetry simultaneously responds to the romance of language (as intricate formal game) and recalls dodgy, carnal, casual, violent political realities which underlie language; it is a poetry of "words and sticks and stones." '12th October, 1994', for instance, marks the eve of a declared Loyalist ceasefire and questions the huge amount of violent amusement available for 20p. Poems like 'Killynether' take us through a new wardrobe door where the world is strange, the self is strange and language is strangest of all.

12th October, 1994

I enter the Twilight Zone,
      the one run
by Frankie 'Ten Pints' Fraser, and slide the heptagon
      of my twenty
pence piece into its slot. The lights come on.
      Sam the Sham
and the Pharaohs are playing *Wooly Bully.*

A virtual combat zone lights up the green
      of my eyes,
my hand clammy on the joystick, as Johnny 'Book
      Keeper' McFeeter
saunters in and Smokey sings *The Tracks of My Tears.*
      He gives the nod
to Betty behind the bulletproof screen.

Love of my life, he says, and she says,
      ach Johnny,
when who do you know but Terry 'The Blaster' McMaster
      levels in
and B Bumble and the Stingers start playing *Nut Rocker.*
      I shoot down
a sniper and enter a higher level.

Betty buzzes Frankie who has a shifty
      look around,
poking his nut around a big blue door, through which
      I spy
Billy 'Warts' McBreeze drinking tea and tapping his toes
      to Randy
and the Rainbows' version of *Denise.*

On the screen I mutilate a double-agent
      Ninja and collect
a bonus drum of kerosene. *Game of Love* by Wayne
      Fontana pumps

out of the machine, when I have to catch my breath,
        realizing Ricky
'Rottweiler' Rice is on my left

saying watch for the nifty fucker
        with the cross-
bow on the right. Sweat-purls tease my spine, tensed ever
        more rigidly,
when Ricky's joined by Andy 'No Knees' Tweed,
        both of them
whistling merrily to The Crystals' *Then He Kissed Me.*

What the fuck is going on
        here, asks
Victor 'Steel Plate' Hogg, as he slides through the fire
        door. The kid's
on level 3, says Andy. At which point Frankie does his nut,
        especially since
The Cramps are playing *Can Your Pussy Do the Dog?*

Betty puts on Curtis and the Clichés'
        Brush Against Me
Barbarella instead, when the first helicopter shreds the air
        to the left
of the screen. Gathering my wits and artillery, I might eclipse
        the high score
of Markie 'Life Sentence' Prentice, set on October 6th.

I hear Benny 'Vindaloo' McVeigh say,
        right we're going
to do this fucking thing. By now the smoke is so thick
        the screen is almost grey.
The Shangri-Las are playing *Remember (Walkin' in the Sand).*
        Frankie says
no, Victor, nobody's going to fucking disband.

Bob B Soxx and the Blue Jeans are playing
        Zip-A-Dee-Doo-Dah.
Through a napalm blur I set the interns free. They wear US

marine khaki.
Jimmy 'Twelve Inch' Lynch says, son, not bad for 20p.
      I leave the Zone and go
back to the fierce grey day. It looks like snow.

Cold Flow

Presley is singing *In the Ghetto*. The sky is almost blue.
Belfast, under blankets of snow, lies like a letter
not yet written. You aim a cigarette, as though it were a
    snooker cue,
at the red ball of her lips. Which never tasted better.
The hill path is glazed with rippled glass, and you gaze through
a frozen sea of trees, at the town's oyster-bedded pearl,
while smoke fudges the lough like a Cadbury's Twirl™.

While smoke fudges the lough like a Cadbury's Twirl™,
you see colour-fleck cars and butterfly people sprinkling
their hundreds and thousands across the soft icing roads,
    thinking
of singing to Elvis. But she turns away, as if to say how stinking
the snow will become. What a whizz. What a whirl. What a
    girl.
So clever. So bitter. You could have hit her. The sky-dome
    douses
whipped-cream snow, coating the strawberry brick of houses.

Whipped-cream snow coats the strawberry brick of houses,
while aeroplanes levitate like Aero Bars™ over the tip
edge of Belfast's fruit bowl. The sweet snow flies as the
    cloudless
sky cries, and you wipe your runny nose as the cold wind
    blows.

It was the cigarette that tasted good. Not her strawberry lips.
She is melting into the horizon's bones, and as an aeroplane
    drones,
desiccated coconut flakes fall on your face that turns toward
    home.

Desiccated coconut flakes fall on your face, turned toward
    home
laid out like a blanket, through trees that are ice-cream cones.
The melting path sparkles like a Genuine American Miller™
bottle. And 100,000 butterflies will die, jealous of caterpillars,
while flowers ignite themselves in protest, then surrender
to the infinite cold flow, icing the Milky Way through.
Presley is singing *In the Ghetto*. The sky is almost blue.

To Belfast

May your bulletproof knickers drop like rain
and your church-spires attain a higher state of grace.
My lily-of-the-valley, the time is at hand
to ring your bells and uproot your cellulose stem.
I bought hardware, software, and binoculars to trace
your ways of taking the eyes from my head.

And none of it worked. We've been coming to a head
for too long; aircraft prick the veins of your rainbow as they shoot you in soft focus to trace
the tramlines of your cellulite skin. But with the grace
of a diva on a crackling screen, you never stem
to their cameras, you're forever getting out of hand.

Once in school, on a greaseproof page, we had to trace
the busts and booms of your body, and I was ashamed to hand
mine in because it lacked what Da called grace.
And I wish I was the centre of a rain-
drop that's falling on your head, the key to your handcuffs, the drug that could re-conjugate your head.

For Belfast, if you'd be a Hollywood film, then I'd be Grace
Kelly on my way to Monaco, to pluck the stem
of a maybell with its row of empty shells, its head
of one hundred blinded eyes. I would finger your trace
in that other city's face, and bite its free hand
as it fed me, or tried to soothe the stinging of your rain.

Don't You

I

I was working as a waitress in a cocktail bar,
that much is true. But even then I knew I'd find
myself behind the wheel of a large automobile,
or in a beautiful house, asking myself, well,
if sweet dreams are made of these, why don't I travel
the world and the seven seas to Rio, and dance there
in the sand, just like a river twisting through the dusty land?
For though you thought you were my number one,
this girl did not want to have a gun for hire,
no bright spark who was just dancing in the dark.

II

You were working as a waitress in a cocktail bar,
when I met you. And I believed in miracles:
every step you took, I was watching you.

I asked for your name, tipped you again and again
and you said, Don't - don't you want me
to fetch you a drink that would turn your pink mouth blue?
Don't you think this tenth tiny chaser is ten times bigger
    than you?
Don't you talk about places and people you will never know.
Don't you symbolize femininity by use of the letter O.
And I said, Don't you want me, baby? Don't you want me...

Last Friday Night

So there wi were like, on the fuckin dance
floor an the skank was fuckin stormin like,
shite-posh, but we'd fuckin chance
it, great big fuckin ditties bouncin, shite,
an thighs, skirts wi fuckin arses man, tight,
that ye'd eat yer fuckin heart out fer. I
was fuckin weltered an Victor was ripe
aff his head cos we'd been round wi Johnny
like, downin the duty-free fuckin gargle, aye.

Anyway, wee Markie must've taken
a few a tha aul disco biscuits like,
loved up da fuck, goin like a mad yin
when some dicklicker came over like, for a fight.
Slabberin! So the fuckin lads go 'right!'
an a huge fuckin mill-up started but
I fucked aff when this tit's head cracked aff a light.
Fuck sake like, my knuckles are still cut.
Shame ye wernie there, ya nut.

Killynether

Each time I ignore the stranger in the mirror
on the big wardrobe door, and open wide
its lacquered hatches, lured by the whiff
of dark hanging coats, their Crave and Regal
and their black Quink ink, rubbing my face into
bakeries and florists, the sweat of city buses,

I find another row of jackets where no row could be,
and walk onwards into leather and denim,
limited edition LPs, Lynn or Suzie pouting from empty
Tennant's lager tins, drawing me further into blazers,
football boots and Tupperware lunches,
until eventually, I walk onto Killynether.

At such times I curse my limited imagination.
But then I notice the colour of the grass,
its wet hair hum, and the underworld of tree trunks
and bluebells, the '99' clouds kiss-curling
from Comber to Croob, the peninsula's finger,
and it dawns on me I never knew the names

of ladies' smock or orange tips, the meadow
browns and ringlets; I never walked among
the celandine, silverweed, wood sage and clover;
never listened to the stonechats and linnets,
the stocking creepers fluttering over green-winged
orchids, twayblades, samphire, or elder;

I never caught my shirt on a blazing hedge's
billhooks, by the blackthorn and dogwood,
gliding the breeze with the turnstones and terns,
hawking drumlins and pladdies, following wagtails
and warblers towards Jackdaw Island,
or Darragh Island by Ringhaddy Sound;

I never savoured the wave splash and salt spray,
the sandhoppers feeding on the strandline;
the horse mussels, bulrushes and lugworm casts,
shelducks, oystercatchers, widgeon and snipe
preying on the knotted wrack and eel-grass;
I was never entangled in dense forests of kelp;

I was never dragged beneath the surface
by velvet swimming crabs, to submarine
sand dunes with star pokers and dog cockles
or burrowing brittlestars; I never swam with thornback
rays or nurse hounds to the currents of the Narrows,
coming to rest with anemones and coral.

It's been years since I walked through Killynether.
When I wake I wonder if I've been there ever.
Sometime I must, before I flick the screen
and set about my business, or pick up the telephone,
wander over to the big lacquered wardrobe and open
negotiations with the stranger in the mirror.

Progress

They say that for years Belfast was backwards
and it's great now to see some progress.
So I guess we can look forward to taking boxes
from the earth. I guess that ambulances
will leave the dying back amidst the rubble
to be explosively healed. Given time,
one hundred thousand particles of glass
will create impossible patterns in the air
before coalescing into the clarity
of a window. Through which, a reassembled head
will look out and admire the shy young man
taking his bomb from the building and driving home.

Aries

One day you might start, poke your crack
and finally dawn on yourself, and climb
out of your sleepy head hollow,
catching a grip to fling wide the peachy
curtains, the stripes on your back
the healing fingers of the blind.

And you might well get up and go,
and tiptoe through this doorway forever,
sashaying through the neverland gardens
by lady's fingers and foxtails, the flushed
tormentils and archangels, tattoos of fritillaries,
Mars burning in the floribunda's glow.

In a nostalgic lapse, you might begin praying
for viral spreads, gnarls, rented alibis
and secret butchers, the avenues and alleyways,
turpentine and zippo, digital eyes preying
on elevator cord-snaps, freak-outs on the motorway,
the fall and phantom lustre of her eyes.

But forget all that, for you will be rolling
with the speedwells and ghost orchids
in your dizzybells and superlation,
the garden spooling into an ever-zooming
city of corundum domes and almandine spires,
the discombobulation of dandillies looming

in souped-up Subarus with their hullaballoo;
and with a rat-a-tat-tat in your temples will you
savour the salt of crizzled skin on your tongue,
the console of your eyes mounting through
the avenues and alleyways, where you will thrive
with shock and awe in the gash of the sun.

There

Scooshing by barrels in brewers' yards,
by the Enterprise ratcheting southward;
spanging over downs of such avocado green
you check yourself, and through elmwood demesnes
that canopy civil servants in the twilight;
scooshing the dark between bulbs of light
pollution, past lynchets, bales, and unstill horses,
the rain-soaked lough, the detachment of houses;

slacken at the clutter of an outspilling town:
there smoke flues and scaffolding, run down
chemists and redevelopment clearance sites,
car parks and faded posters of kick boxing fights
occupy hooded teens, the question marks
of their clusters, their murmur more dark
than passers-by can account for, on their way to
late night malls, the news, convenience drive-throughs -

the till ka-chinging demographic, who'd like to cycle
more in the future, who drive miles to recycle
and buy organic, passing value-pack fish fingers
purchased for scuzzed children, whose eyes linger
on the shelf-bright colours, leaving by flexi-bus
for estates on the outskirts, complexes of window dust
beyond the cctv zones, where high-walled shadows
veil adjoining green fields, their symmetrical hedgerows

revealing the depth of order. There Way Out signs
rust quietly. There dead leaves bare the trees' design,
thornbushes sharpen, militant jackdaws shiver
on thin wires, policing the lash-cackled river;
and past a station post, its generator's hum,
the loughside sluices pebbles, an ulcered tongue
slithered over rent teeth. There you must earn your living:
locked in food-chains, frigid skylines unforgiving.

In her Room on a Light-Kissed Afternoon

Not only the nip and tuck of her skin quilting
milk bent bones; not only the somersaulting
head spin of her light-pelted skin spread atilt
the deep of her lemon-puffed pillow and quilt
lifting into the citron-charged air; but even the lilt
of strings from the speaker on her well-built
mockernut cabinet, the light from her half-
opened window, and the high heckled laugh
of girls promenading past her bedroom,
scrickety-screeching over each other's lampoon
of a pizza-faced boy they tortured all afternoon;
even the snow-capped peaks of her importune
shoulder-bones, the squidged soles of her feet,
the daylight's tufts in the meadowsweet
sky charged with godwits, lemon-pufffed billows
and Boeings: all these things sink below
her ass-through-mouth fear of the aeroplane's *kaboom,*
its flaring nose dive-bombing her bedroom;
her fear of turning cloud, her skin become cotton,
a lemon-puffed pastry shred to pieces in the rotten
sky and windblown, turned into tears
cut like arrowheads, salt-fired and clear,
pitter-patter-clattering her window
as I plunge into her lip-stained pillow
and quilt of her light citrus skin
with hate mail, emissions, election results breaking in
as we lie there, beating, dead to our bones
in her lemon-puffed bower of words, and sticks, and stones.

Paul Grattan

Paul Grattan was born in Glasgow, Scotland, in 1971. He graduated from Strathclyde University, moved to the North of Ireland in 1995 and completed an M.A. in Creative Writing from Lancaster University at The Poets' House, County Antrim. He has been a writer in residence at Flax Art Studios (Belfast). Currently living in Dublin, he is Academic Manager of an English language school and lectures on University College Dublin's Adult Education Programme. His first poetry collection is *The End of Napoleon's Nose* (Edinburgh Review, 2002).

In Paul Grattan's poetry the mock and deadly serious are a stone's throw away; a balance of under, and over, statement power many poems. The poetry is a meld of Glaswegian-Belfast "speak", philosophy, photography, Scottish literature, Hiberno-English, soccer reportage and brand names; the linguistic clanjamfrie does not feel forced; the poetry is acutely aware of the physical or political freight that words carry. A welter of dictions are "held hostage" without "bad faith" in the organic unity of poems which deftly enact mercurial shifts and collisions in puns or ironies as they migrate between "high" and "low" culture or art. The poems point to junctures and disjunctures between working class life and radical thought in Ulster and Scotland. There is the link between poverty and history (captured by photography) or poverty and ill temper (the proximity of poor rations and rashers and second hand clothes) in one of mid-Ulster's greasy spoons. In 'Descartes at Ibrox' both epistemological method and sectarian fists connect to "insist on their existence". The poet dons "the hospital gown of (his) own style" in a sequence of poems to test the powerlessness of seriously ill patients (and visitors) against the power of doctors and to reveal their relative powerlessness in a health service in terminal decline. The sheer brutality of 'Pipe Dream' interrogates any claim poetry might make as a self-enclosed arena or transcendent medium, while a poem like 'Middle' balances fondness and pithy socio-political commentary in a blend of great delicacy and power. It is indeed "curious" the way in which this poetry tunes its ear to combining a "skeptical temperament" with "buffoonery or calculation" so that Marx or metaphysics rub shoulders with trousers or fish suppers in the adventure.

Maxim

in memory of Hywel Thomas, philosopher

And if we should be refused trousers
or find ourselves foutering under stars,
exiled by grocers' daughters, in Cuban
heels, a high-heel without curves, better
to have been tarred and feathered in the great
balloon fire of 1785 than suffer this closure,
half out of our patent leathered minds.

You kill me, roaring, tautologies of fuchsia
and blackthorn have emptied our bellies,
binding our hyperborean arse cracks to the wind.
My manqué, my melancholic manqué, go on
in your virtue, save the wails, the wind eggs
and a thousand dule-tree flowers, for the want
of a kind word, John Knox looking on.

No Second Fry, Cookstown, February 24th 2000

She too eschews a surface patience, preparing to chew
in dentured indigence her buttered stick of soldiers,
having first arranged two sausage on a side-plate. Isabel's
café and clothes shop combined. Behind the hot glass
lurk rashers, great lobes of grease curled inwards

in coronary prayer. Eggs stare igneous and jaundiced
as beans bake on their own ring, pushed beyond use,
a callus against appetite. Downstairs my wife is fishing
for tights in bargain buckets. I barter my boiled tomato,
a last isosceles of soda bread surpassing expectations.

Buried under a stew of pramless mothers, her blue rinsed
coral plateau takes the biscuit. You might think images
of ageing would be less frivolous - lines of mean winter
tempered with equal amounts of sunshine - instead, ah
Isabel, caustic in rancid knickers, waiting for Ostend to fall.

In Situ
from A Typical Cell

A nurse has taken pity and the time to find me
coffee, while they prep you for the table with a
viscous yellow rub. Surgeon and Anaesthetist
differ on the risk you pose expensive, fraught
procedures and the limits to your blood. At half-

past three a plastic screen is circled round your
morphined lids. A junior Doctor waves her gold
tipped nib across some document and inks out
a release. Morphine signs on your behalf then
dandles down two tubers, protruding from your wrist

and middle finger. Swabs of artificial light
decline an article I read on *Cancer and You, the facts.*
Freesias someone left you wither at the window
like they want to get out and I can't kiss you
for catheters, stinking, waiting to be fixed.

The Seven Rabbie Burns's Bad Faith Come Back Tour

*His ill-fitting, glossy black cloth, ungainly presence and sharp, dark vulpine
features had in them the vulgarity of a Glasgow artisan in his Sabbath suit.*
                    - from Uncle Silas, by Sheridan le Fanu

We never really knew exactly who was being held hostage
or why, synchronised, we sang in the accent of the captor

opening the heart of Andreas Baader. As if we birled to kiss
the cross the day they took out brother Ross, the Guinness Book

of Records gawping openly that next night on the News at Ten.
Full of Eastern Promise, we played support to The Thanes of Lauder

during the rain of the Year of Culture. The greatest hit
we never had, a cover off Steak & Kidney's *Govan Cross* L.P.,

Seven Syllables' On The Death Of Deng Xiao Ping.
We like to call it, Sweet And Sour Balls Gone Tae Seed.

Pipe Dream

Daft bastard never realised you could hear fuck all
for the noise of the lathe, his luck turning at eighteen hundred revs,
a fool on a rough feed ripping chunks out of a democratically
elected Communist government - *Get aff the soap the box ya clown,
these X's 'll burn your fuckin eyes out* - a worthless gesture,
grating against the bight of the chuck, the perspex faceguard
smothering all congress. We stopped the feed, pulled back
the cross slide freeing the fool and switched off the machine.

Then I felt we had betrayed him, in the rubble of the Moneda,
a sell-out crowd for the end of season game - *At least play
tae the whistle, brother, if ye canny write tae the bone.*
If you ask them in La Legua, Victor Jara should go home.

Swarfega'd palms sud memories of a wee, decent man
whose Party we compared with the Sunday Post - *shite paper* -
three days later his neck struck our hard logic and snapped,
the pipe still in his hand. His soul arced through the air,
showering us both with hot ash.

Descartes at Ibrox
for Martin Mooney

Check him, some waster waxing lyrical in a bar,
chinned by a bear in Rangers colours for failing
to hum ardently the air to Derry's Walls; this *per se*
would not seem unusual. Except it didn't happen

Qua rammy. Injuries were sustained as a result
of paper cuts to the left nostril, inflicted when said Hun
proclaimed Hume's rebuttal of the French Man to be
epistemologically speaking, *fucking out of order.*

Coming to, reverse angle replays show two tattooed
fists insist on their existence, above and beyond the temple
of the Copeland Road Stand. Man marked, out the game
the upward trajectory of his meditations proved fatal.

A Marxist Sends a Postcard Home
from A Little Night Music - for Innes Kennedy

Last night they took our drainpipe for the bonfire
and it's only May - which just goes to show uncle Tam

knew hee-haw about seasonal politics. So now rain
rivets the pavement instead of trickle-down. Rats rave
in the attack to the helicopter's three a.m. arias
and the party in my head won't stop. *Who will raise
a glass to our broken faces and see this place?*

When we were weans I chased her campaign Ford
Cortina round the cottage flats and semi's of Croftfoot.
Election night in Donegal Pass brings back the way
you lashed an aspirant 'h' between the 'c' and 'u' of 'cunt'
whenever talking Tory. We both have drunk and downward
dragged the deeply bearable. Nudged now towards
new labours, we'd better work our better halves to death.

The End of Napoleon's Nose
from A Little Night Music

Tonight we are folding our sins into newspaper,
drowning our chips in malt vinegar from ginger bottles
outside the Golden Sea. The naturally saturated high
of fish suppers in transit, nasal napalm for the blind.

At the back of the mind, dole-queues swell like poppers,
trips liquefy shelf lives in showers of six o'clock shoppers.
We lick fingers, salty from other fuckers' wounds, testing
The products' unfamiliar skin. Impeccably dressed

for the price of a can we might kill the horsey-set pigs -
a scene out of Dostoevsky - black tongued Bulgarian wine
drinkers' sons in combat boots with flak-jacket faces
dragging a donkey down the waterworks to see if it floats.

Belfast fills with ghosts. Greyhounds' sport coats to keep
the dogma out. We toss and dream of ice-cream, the virtues
of dirty women, until solvent at last, its time to pick
one half of eglantine, at the end of Napoleon's nose.

Aisling

for Joe Woods

Leave a long butt, the warning tells you.
Remove from mouth between yawning
and if you must inhale less, take fewer
puffs, even compose reasons for giving
up the only source of light in your ashtray.

Middle

from The Municipal Family Revisited

In Gran's house, a plastic swan from Saltcoats kept
watch inside the alcove. Wings made bouquets of daffodils
phlegm-quilled in their yellowed dustcoat plume.

Well-fired morning rolls would hatch from white
paper bags like dinosaur eggs, in the Ladybird books
she read me. Two halves of breakfast, *brake* and

fast, forever severed by the standard Habbie of her
tongue. *Elizabeth the first of Scotland and her retinue
dropped by the Barrhead Road around the time yon toe-rag*

Teddy Taylor was in Castlemilk. With the clarity of one
who has abdicated motor functions, she minds the Corpy
planting silver birch, skin-deep in tar-macadam.

Kerry Hardie

Kerry Hardie was born in 1951 in Singapore. She grew up in County Down, worked for the BBC in Northern Ireland in the 1970s, based in Derry, and returned there a few years ago for a writer's residency in the Verbal Arts Centre, during the Bloody Sunday Tribunal. She currently lives in Kilkenny. Kerry Hardie has written a novel entitled *Hannie Bennet's Winter Wedding* (Harper Collins, 2000) and a second novel, *The Bird Woman*, is forthcoming. Her three collections of poetry are *A Furious Place* (Gallery Press, 1996), *Cry for the Hot Belly* (Gallery Press, 2000) and *The Sky Didn't Fall* (Gallery Press, 2003).

The poetry collections of Kerry Hardie follow the seasons in a mainly rural setting; there is a clear eye for telling, symbolic detail and the townland textures that underlie the big official map. Times and places are re-mapped to posit philosophical or human questions that arise from the ways we are inextricably enmeshed within the cycle of birth, growth, suffering and death. Elemental forces, life and mortality, are "deep in the life" of the poetry which acts as an anatomy of the human heart as both a tender and "furious place… so raw, so pure and so shameless". The poetry also answers to John Hewitt's image of "moth that answers moth"; it is aware that all our tenderness may be "No more than the weight/of a blink of the moth's eye"; this awareness of suffering and death underpins a humane poem like 'Cry for the Hot Belly'. The poetry asks questions about the limits or existence of human or divine power. In 'The Avatar', for instance, the poet asks whether a friend's definition of the trinity as "God the curlew, God the eider,/God the cheese-on-toast" is adequate in the face of "awe". When the poetry explores political questions or the North it does so with a genuine modesty that refuses the soap-box or trite omniscient explanations in favour of a longer term awareness of our inescapable subjectivity and mortality. If the poem is imagined as a "flag" at all then it is one of "songs/of dream or prayer". Indeed a key feature of much of this poetry is its liberal ability to explore human, and by extension political, relationships from diverse viewpoints; we look through the eyes of husbands, wives, childless women, bachelors, sisters and brothers as well as mothers, fathers and daughters.

We Change the Map

This new map, unrolled, smoothed,
seems innocent as the one we have discarded,
impersonal as the clocks in rows
along the upper border, showing time-zones.

The colours are pale and clear, the contours
crisp, decisive, keeping order.
The new names, lettered firmly, lie quite still
within the boundaries that the wars spill over.

It is the times.

I have always been one for paths myself.
The mole's view. Paths and small roads and the next bend.
Arched trees tunnelling to a coin of light.
No overview, no sense of what lies where.

Pinning up maps now, pinning my attention,
I cannot hold whole countries in my mind,
nor recognise their borders.

These days I want to trace
the shape of every townland in this valley;
name families; count trees, walls, cattle, gable-ends,
smoke-soft and tender in the near blue distance.

The Farm Girl Remembers Home
for Heather

She spoke of that birthday,
of stories, one on another,
leaf drifting on leaf.
She spoke for a lost life,
for her own heart's yearning
now that she lives
outside the walls.

She spoke as one looking
on night-starry skies
when we are grown leaf-thin, violable,
and the high dreams float about our heads
and press through our waking selves;
her eyes, helpless and rapt,
watching herself dissolve.

What was she, only a country girl
in city trappings,
the gee-gaws in her ears
his fairings given her in some Glasgow bar?
Taking the pins from her crowned head,
letting the hair fall loose,
she could have been anyone's 'Brown Colleen,
The star of the County Down'.

It wasn't a happiness that had been,
and now was lost, in a city full of cries.
Only the bright squared quilts
spread airing in the yard.
The rest was tear-trails
down an ashey childhood.
It was a longing for her place,
to know her task, fend off this loneliness.

Listening, I was that, too;
I wanted to go back behind the walls
where I had lived and never lived,
to be again the peaty loam
and listen, sodden through womb ears,
to ancient dark-brown dreams,
leaf singing unto leaf,
stained water to stained light.

Siblings

*The Derryman told of the childhood holiday in the village in Donegal and how
he had gone with his father and caught a fish and had carried it home through
the blue evening; and the pride of it, greeting people and them knowing, and his
mother ready at the stove to cook it. How they had eaten the fish and it had lived
inside him for years and years, as Jonah lived in the whale, only the other way
round, and then when he was grown with a son of his own he went back to the
village and there was no river in it or near it or flowing past it, no river at all.*

I

There was a fish but no river
there was no river so there was no fish
there *was* a fish whether or not there was a river
and if there was a fish there *must* have been a river -
and anyway there was the blue evening
not to mention his father's hand on his shoulder.

II

We are always there, you and I, at the table
leaning forward, our elbows together
and our feet braced, our hands locked
and our eyes locked, and I do not know
any of the people crowding dimly
around us as we sit, implacable
at the fulcrum of our clasped hands,
ready at any moment
to force down the other's arm.

We argue, my brother, of fishes, of rivers,
yet you have pulled fish and I have pulled fish
thudding onto the bank, heaving, shining,
from the river that was no river.

The Cruellest Month
for Bernadette Kiely

We came round the bent road in the drowned light
of a Spring evening
and I saw you, in your dark coat,
your hair dark, your face white, your hands full of lilacs -

You might have been a bride, the way you walked,
your head high, him beside you, but separate,
like a woman coming from the church a hundred years ago,
going home with the man, to begin the life contracted.

It was all lit
from elsewhere: the stormy evening, the white light,
the small squat houses, the river running black
by the stone quays, the chestnuts climbing.

And those lilacs, a mass of them,
spreading out of your hands:
a white one, a mauve one, a white one -
Not casual. Some eye deciding, some hand arranging
the eye's bidding.

All week I'd been on about lilacs,
had stood by a window in the evening looking down
on a lilac in the garden, its few blooms
with the reddish stain of blood behind their purple -

Those famous lines were in my mind, this being the month,
but it wasn't right - his lilacs, not our lilacs.
Our lilacs: out of a green land, some with blood on their
    roots.
And white ones, planted by the Marian grottos.
And mauve, plebeian, by the ruined gable ends.

These lilacs, drawn to your hands
like the thought-forms of flowers;
their fall over your hands, down the dark coat,
their thick scent on the chilly air.

You by the quay, walking another century,
as though our dramas act and re-enact on the same stage,
so that I saw you,
and a woman that had gone before you,
and lilacs, clustering into your hands from hers.

Covenant

The grid of ribbed light sliding under the water
as the full tide slides into the little stream-cut creaks.
The blue rib of the storm-broken boat.

*

The high arching of ribs over the slack belly
of the dun cow lain on the rushy grass
in the washed morning light, the storm spent.

*

The ribbed arc of sprung bone
of the fish on the river path,
the belly eaten away, the ribs rising to shield it.

*

How the ribs rise everywhere
over the hot, soft belly;
how I, seeing everywhere,
high life collapsing into death,

walk here by the black-plumed reed
ribbed with the purple of loosestrife,
cry for the hot belly
gone from the bleaching bone.

Carthage

Lying beside you,
my hand on your sleeping,
feeling your life,
a pulse of light round the skin.

Lying beside you,
your strong bones, dense flesh.
This life-thing. No more than the weight
of a blink of the moth's eye.

Things That are Lost

My mother teaches me the fading skills:
how to clean fish, plait garlic, draw pheasants;
how to distinguish wading birds,
how to make linen lace.

I know her ache because it is in me.
I try to teach anyone who'll listen
wild flowers: their legends, properties, names.
I do this in full love of the fresh world.

But a voice says,
Lose things, forget them, let them go.
See all things always the first time.
Unnamed. In wonder.

Mother, in Age

like weather that's always
busy about the place, filling
the long pond, warming
the near pavement, feathering
grasses in the upper field -

Now she has stripped the leaves
she has ice-flowered
the water in the barrel, and I
wind my horn through her falling snow
against the hushed stillness

of its lying.

On Derry's Walls

'A thing can be explained only by that which is more subtle than itself; there is
nothing subtler than love: by what then can love be explained?'
        - Sumnûn ibn Hamza al-Muhibb

The blackbird that lives in the graveyard
sits on the Wall at the fade of the winter day.
He has fed off the worms that have fed off the clay
of the Protestant dead.

And yet he is subtle,
subtle and bright
as the love that might explain him
yet may not be explained.

As for the rest, there is almost nothing to add,
not even *This is how it was,*
because all we can ever say
is *This is how it looked to me -*

In the blackbird's looped entrails
everything is resolved.

Day's Ending

We quiet ourselves, expecting the night.
We have left ourselves, await ourselves,
in this place between. Life moves
in the room, becomes more itself
each moment we let it alone.

This, our best chance
at absence while present,
the time we least feel
our weight pressing in on us.

We long for this,
yet cannot bear it for long.
One of us always
rises, walks over, turns on the lights.

John Hughes

John Hughes was born in Belfast in 1962. He was educated at Queen's University (where he studied English and Scholastic Philosophy) and at the University of Ulster. He has lived in New York and currently lives in County Donegal. His collections of poems are *The Something in Particular* (Gallery Press, 1986), *Negotiations with the Chill Wind* (Gallery Press, 1991), *The Devil Himself* (Gallery Press, 1996) and *Fast Forward* (Lagan Press, 2003).

This poetry asks unflinching questions, uses exactingly honed assertions and precise, shocking images to illuminate dark arenas of public and private life and their interaction. Dogs, usually symbols of domestic affection or national loyalty, are often dead; wardrobes double as barricades; a lamb morphs into a wolf. The poetry forges a strange, original, deliberately unstable meld of film, philosophy and fantasy to interrogate public appearance and inner nightmare. The deceptively casual voice and blackly humorous tone also act as a foil for lacerating precision and honesty which uncover the impact of religion and political mayhem on the psyche. Poems often have a strange capacity to present subversive, unanswerable, riddles and direct parables at one and the same time. If we are taken into a world where anything can, and literally does, happen amidst the perverse mayhem and violence then it is also a world where these forces are integral to the serious content, tone or formal, reflective structures adopted by each poem. From 'Porn' (whose fat man knows "none of us can have all we want -/in this neck of the woods" where "an indiscretion is never missed/and the smallest offence/is almost always taken/to the most ridiculous lengths") through to 'What Makes Its Way in Darkness Ends' (with its bleak historical analysis of a place that throws up martyrs when it needs men), the devastating ironies and mercury tilt of imagery point their lance at more than windmills. In some ways this poetry forms a verbal parallel to the visual art of Northern painters like Martin Wedge and Dermot Seymour who have explored both outer terror and inner damage through, respectively, heightened expressionism or the surreal that shades into the hyper-real.

Porn

The fat man had called round
once too often for comfort;
his fascination for Maureen
was getting on my nerves.

I'd been hospitable till
he asked to be alone with her;
basically he was a lecher
with a sad, sad face.

He was hamming it up
well past his bedtime,
causing pain and sorrow
beyond anything I'd experienced

since the night Citizen Lumière
had re-possessed the camera
and left me in the dark
as to its rightful owner.

But I'd tell the fat man
none of us can have all we want
in this neck of the woods -
where the light is so perfect

an indiscretion is never missed
and the smallest offence
is almost always taken
to the most ridiculous lengths.

A Respect for Law and Order
for Dermot Seymour

The general will be shot in the face
when his new chauffeur forgets orders
and stops for a red traffic-light.
Within the hour one of the usual suspects
will be rounded up and taken downtown
to an interrogation room on the tenth floor
of the National Central Security building;
and after five hours of electric shocks
and beatings with a length of rubber-hose
he will be ordered to open the window
and step outside for a breath of fresh air.

He will fall head-first onto a crowded pavement
of journalists, pickpockets, private detectives,
air-force pilots, French polishers, jazz-guitarists,
civil servants in the Department of Information,
elderly women on their way across town
to visit their latest grandchild,
young men sauntering to a soccer match
between the national side and Paraguay,
a famous Italian new expressionist painter,
and the newly-arrived cultural attaché
of the Republic of South Africa.

The suspect will then pick himself up,
take a look at himself in the nearest window,
tuck in his shirt, straighten his tie,
and disappear into the leafy suburb
where he lives in a modest apartment
with his second wife and her two children;
and finish the book he was reading
when interrupted by an old schoolfriend
dressed to the nines in a uniform
he had recently come to respect.

Diesel

One blue mountain road zigs and the other zags
before they entwine to become the road
to Jack Gallagher's MS station.

Driving along that road in a chunky 4 X 4 -
on my way to buy gallon upon gallon of diesel
and half a hundredweight of Blues and Pinks -

I listened to the devils' stories
about Ardoyne, Iberian griffins, desert frost,
and bishops who sweat semen in their sleep.

It was driving Kerrys and Jerseys along the same road
that the angels told my grandfather
stories about the fifth apostle and Munster Simms.

When the angels disappeared behind a Famine wall
my grandfather coughed up his ravaged lungs
and threw them to the winged lion

that had been stalking him for fifty years -
from the time he set fire to a Red Kelly barn
built to store the fleece of the Lamb of God.

*

The lion swooped down on me
as I poured gallon upon gallon of diesel
over the Blues and the Pinks, the devils and the angels.

Leaving Home

The day I threw my head up and left home
my mother told me the facts of life:

Catholicism is based on opium
and mutual masturbation,

the Garden of Eden is submerged
beneath the Caspian Sea,

the Holy Ghost was born in County Offaly,

from Cape Verde to the Cape of Good Hope
all exchanges and valuations of merchandise
are made on the foot of the macoute,

the pygmies of Thrace are born aged five
and die aged eight.

*

And if these facts lead me to believe
a king is not a king
a yard from his throne,
who can say it's easier
to forget where we've come from
than to remember where we're going to?

Blood

When I said she smelt of a lamb and a wolf
she coughed up the field she was born in.
I knew she believed me to be Christ of March 25th.

How often have I walked through the town of Dungiven
flanked by a wolf-headed lamb and a lamb-headed wolf -
the blood coming from their wounds mine and mine alone.

The Dark Oaks Stayed Strangely Still

I knew how much fear was in my father
When he took me aside after the rosary

And said, 'That I was the terror of that woman
Was the most natural thing in the world.'

Like the coward I was I said nothing,
And set off to burn the soiled bedlinen

Beyond the dark oaks that hold the house in shadow,
Be there winter sun or summer rain.

Such an absurd day. A dog lay at the foot of the bed,
Listening to the corpse's putrefying innards groan and growl.

Snow swirled in from the moon-blanched glen.
Neighbours made their way through the dark oaks

To the bedside of one dressed in the blue garments of Mary,
Of one who'd cried and screamed and prayed -

As if that could stop the uncontrollable shitting,
Drooling and puking.

And I wondered how long I would have to stay
In the country of winter's dregs, of spectral grey.

All around the house the Donegal wind twisted and turned,
And yet, and yet, the dark oaks stayed strangely still.

The Brains of the Operation

In the course of hunting feral cats and wounded foxes,
Driving tanker-loads of diesel and van-loads of *Embassy Regal*,
I cross the border a hundred times a day.

At Lifford, I rest beneath the oaks till noon,
At Killea, I pull rushes from under the feet of old men,
On Clady bridge I swallow the pebbles that line my pockets.

Ever since I witnessed my barber being shot in the head
By a retard whose hair he'd cut since the age of seven,
I have believed 32 is a magical number.

I can wake in a ditch with a thousand pounds in my pocket
And know nothing of how they came to be there.
I'm a rare creature for I can smell blood from a mile off.

Often I'm dragged into the back of a Land Rover or Ford Granada
To have my privates twisted and pulled
By slack-jawed peelers who think it a kind of party game.

For a week now I've made camp on the shores of Mullaghmore,
Where I make note of stars that have not been seen
Since the night before Lord Mountbatten went the way of all flesh.

I'm a man who can swallow his own hand,
Who has never told a joke against himself,
Who knows the etymology of *saveloy*.

Pillow Talk

I wake into a dream of biting into your flesh
To discover it tastes like rotten apples,

And raise myself up on one arm to vow yet again
Never ever to drink *Liebfraumilch* by a full moon.

You lie across my chest and ask me question after question:
Who are you? Which one of us smells so bad?

Was it you who threw up in the bath and kitchen sink?
Were you the fucker who wrecked my hi-fi?

As the questions keep coming,
Last night comes back to me little by little:

West of the Bann is ours to have and to hold.
Six pints of Harp and half a bottle of Paddy.

Paddy Reilly murdering 'The Fields of Athenry',
Puking my guts into an avocado bath.

The TV turned up as Big Gerry waves regally
From an armour-plated black taxi.

A DUP poster tossed onto the fire.
Five pints of Smithwicks and half a bottle of Black Bush.

A pair of Trillick shinners saying I wasn't right in the head
When I tried to explain that to remember you must forget.

A strapless dress, bra and tights.
A tangle of arms and legs.

As for your questions, what can I tell you
That you don't already know?

That'll stop you asking again and again
What exactly it was we should never ever have done.

The Wardrobe

Twenty-five years have passed since last I laid eyes
On this battered wardrobe - the Saturday evening
My father hauled it downstairs to barricade the front door.

While his wife and children tossed and turned in their beds,
My father nailed lengths of sweet-smelling 4x2
Across every window on the ground floor.

Come morning, his face was as white as the refrigerator,
He laid a hurley stick on the kitchen table and told me:
Hobgoblin, nor foul fiend, should daunt our spirit.

For hours on end, I watched snow fall on the Oldpark,
Covering Sam McCrum's Hillman Hunter,
The brains of Mrs. Zukor's knocked-down Pomeranian.

Bored with fear, I changed into my mothballed Sunday best,
And in a room dark and quiet as my brain
I waited for our killers to make their way from Silverstream.

On Monday morning the removal men arrived.
I remember so clearly how they dropped the wardrobe
As they lumbered along the icy garden path,

How eagerly I tore the perfect wings from the moths
That came fluttering,
Fluttering out of its stinking darkness.

What Makes Its Way In Darkness Ends in Darkness

It was early dark, in the thick of teeming snowfall,
When we veered off the concession road
To meet a stranger with a familiar face.
I don't deserve this were the only words he spoke
As the hood was put over his close-shaven head.

Would that he'd stayed where he belonged -
In the house built by the gallows tree,
Of the rebels of such and such a year,
And the rebels of such and such a year.
Would that our screams had not become his and his alone.

Nick Laird

Nick Laird was born in 1975 in County Tyrone and attended Cookstown High School. He studied English Literature at Cambridge, went to Law School, has worked as a commercial litigator in the City of London and as a literary journalist. He has lived in Warsaw and Boston and now lives in Kilburn, London, where he writes full-time. *Utterly Monkey* (Fourth Estate, 2005) is Nick Laird's first novel; his first collection of poems is entitled *To a Fault* (Faber, 2005).

This poetry is notable for its great delicacy, ear for language and range: its ability to "mind your language"; its capacity to "calibrate a scale". The poems manage to encompass concise statement and oblique suggestion, the bomb and the noise in the cistern, the precise image and ambivalent pun. The geography of the poems ranges from Tyrone or Donegal to London, Boston and Warsaw. Poems frequently, delicately, manage to counterpoint a tug-of-war between complex emotions: there is the mix of tight-lipped, tactful Ulstermen gathered for a haircut and the blunt décor of a barber's shop where some banter is expected; there is the tug of blood and water, or family and lover, in 'Pedigree' where legal language and suppressed anger wage war; there is the whole notion of "fault" as something that literally saves sweeping the kitchen but which also produces insomnia between partners. An end-of-relationship poem like 'Done' is poised to hover, without closure, between statement and question, a situation akin to some of the Catch 22 situations poems identify in the public sphere in the North: "Riots in Donegal town when they were cleared. / And riots again when they were convicted." A key underlying tension in many poems is that between the instinct for flight or width and the urge to belong or remain; poetry itself is imaged as both a self-reflective view from the top deck of a bus and clear sight from within the family pew at church. Ultimately, in terms of the North, this poetry may be a record of constrictions, violence and tight-lipped principles, of 'Remaindermen' who "hold ideas of north/so singularly brutal that the world/might be ice-bound for good."

Cuttings

Methodical dust shades the combs and pomade
while the wielded goodwill of the sunlight picks out
a patch of paisley wallpaper to expand leisurely on it.

The cape comes off with matador's flourish
and the scalp's washed to get rid of the chaff.
This is the closeness casual once in the trenches

and is deft as remembering when not to mention
the troubles or women or prison.
They talk of parking or calving or missing.

A beige lino, a red barber's chair, one ceramic brown sink
and a scenic wall-calendar of the glories of Ulster
sponsored by JB Crane Hire or some crowd flogging animal feed.

About, say, every second month or so
he will stroll and cross the widest street in Ireland
and step beneath the bandaged pole.

Eelmen, gunmen, the long dead, the police.
And my angry and beautiful father:
tilted, expectant and open as in a deckchair

outside on the drive, persuaded to wait
for a meteor shower, but with his eyes budded shut,
his head full of lather and unusual thoughts.

Poetry

It's a bit like looking through the big window
on the top deck of the number 47.

I'm watching you, and her, and all of them,
but through my own reflection.

Or opening my eyes when everyone's praying.
The wave machine of my father's breathing,

my mother's limestone-fingered steeple,
my sister's tiny fidgets, and me, moon-eyed, unforgetting.

And then the oak doors flapping slowly open to let us out,
like some great injured bird trying to take flight.

The Length of a Wave

At the mythic coast, by the kitchen stove,
my father warms his back and talks of floods,
riptides, the boy drowned in Bundoran.

My mother thinks his moods dependent on the moon,
and this, I think, is a non-trivial thing.
He broke the light switch twice by punching it.

Outside, his voice would echo off John Faulkner's hill
and I could judge the playground's width, the distance
of the storm, by knowing how sound travels.

Now I wait for your letter and get to work late.

This scale I'm calibrating spans from the bomb
to the corpses in the mortuary awaiting recognition.

In between I've notched in other soundings:

the barley banger four fields over,
the gonging of the garage door by tennis balls
then ordinary speech, and under that

an adult seagull's flight, at six or seven feet,
the whispering of next door's cistern,
the tidal breathing of your sleeping,

and a struck match's dry whistle.

Although an ear, I've heard, for resonant frequencies
means one should speak of the droning Chinook,
the domestic slap of the rifle's crack,

systolic summer Lambeg nights, a sea in earshot
of the fields where mushrooms scatter, moon-pale
amazed, like faces upturned to a tidal wave,

because across those miles of hills and dark
the squares of light are quartered flags
hung out to mark the embassies of Home,

where to stay intact's to show your only handsome side -

your back, and where he'd shout from his armchair,
Put your hand to the door. Are you coming in or out?
I'm still not sure. The last flight

would get me back to Donegal by dawn,
to where he nightly watched the sun go down.
I could park and watch light complicate the water,

or wade out through the stinging cold saltwater,
which among its many noted uses
is reputed to be good for cleaning silver,

cutlery, or jewellery, and disinfecting wounds.

The Fault

You woke me and I stood and looked,
astounded, put my foot in it,

withdrew then what I could of it,
'cause come the revolution

of the earth,
the rule is crockery's the first

against the wall,
the reverse of which

I'm rapt with as we each
dissemble sleep, but wait,

and listen to the darkness fidget:
it sucks in its gut, lights up,

and swears under its breath
as it struts through the flat,

unzipping the lino, not stopping
until it's laid down in the slit,

and dared us to watch it,
to hopscotch across its display

of the meanings of cleave,
and accept this is what saves us

from sweeping the kitchen,
and stops us from sleeping.

Remaindermen

Because what I liked about them best
was their ability to thole,
that weathered silence and reluctance,
forenenst the whole damn lot.

They've lived alone for years of course,
and watched their cemeteries filling up
like car parks on a Saturday,
their young grow fat for export.

There are others who know what it is
to lose, to hold ideas of north
so singularly brutal that the world
might be ice-bound for good.

Someone has almost transcribed
the last fifty years of our speech,
and has not once had the chance
to employ the word *sorry*

or press the shift to make the mark
that indicates the putting of a question.
The arch was put wrong this Spring
outside my father's office.

When you enter it states
Safe Home Brethren,
and upon leaving the place
Welcome Here.

The Signpost

Knee-capped on the second Tuesday of the month
by two of the stringy cunts
he'd last bought a round for at Christmas

put paid to the plans for ascending Everest,
and playing for Rangers, even in goal
(though it left open Glentoran, as his father'd suggested).

*

The pistol jammed and they kicked him over.
They could break his legs, they offered,
but he waited, and another gun was brought,

and the barrel held against his calf
(friends, see, so they spared his knees),
and the trigger pulled and the bullet shot.

*

Opening fire: slitting the skin of the side of the flame.
He'd held a bomb the same weight as he'd been when born.
Pan back. Agree with that, the thought he had until he blacked,

what with one arm splayed under, and the other
swung over the blade of his shoulder,
he must, from above, make sense as a signpost.

*

From the Royal's window he got a clear view.
An air vent on a roof lent a heat haze to Belfast,
and two cranes swung their arms low over the city,

as if giving a blessing. Incredible to stay upright
with all that gathered weight. He spied his father's house
but all the lights, strange that, were out.

Pedigree

There are many of us.

My aunt,
the youngest sister,
is a reformed shoplifter.

An uncle breeds champion bantams.

Another, a pig-farmer,
has a racket smuggling cattle
back and forth and back across
the imaginary border.

Me, I've forty-seven cousins.

A scuffle over rustling sheep
became a stabbing in a bar outside Armagh,
and a murderer swings
from a branch high up in our family tree.

Which isn't a willow.

Instead,
an enormous unruly blackthorn hedge,

inside of which a corpse is tangled,
and sags from branch to branch,
like a dewy web:

a farmer jumped on the road, and strangled,
his pockets emptied
of the stock proceeds from the country fair
by two local Roman Catholic farmhands.

Riots in Donegal town when they were cleared.
And riots again when they were convicted.

I may be out on a limb.

One grandfather, the short-horn cattle dealer,
went bankrupt, calmly smoked his pipe,
and died at forty of lung cancer.

Martha, my grandmother, remade Heathhill a dairy farm
and when the rent man came
my mother'd hide behind the sofa with her brothers.

My father spent his boyhood fishing with a hook and
    tinfoil chocolate wrapper.

He coveted a Davy Crockett hat
and shined the medals of his legendary uncles
who'd all died at the Somme,
the Dragoon Guards of Inniskilling.

He left school without sitting his papers
and my mother dropped out to marry him.

Each evening after work and dinner,
she'd do her OU course,
and heave the brown suitcase of books
from out beneath the rickety, mythical bunks
I shared for ten years with my sister.

There is such a shelter in each other.

And you, you pad from the bathroom to Gershwin,
gentled with freckles and moisturized curves,
still dripping, made new, singing your footprints

as they singe the wood floor,
perfect in grammar and posture.

But before you passed me the phone
you were talking, and I couldn't help but note your tone,
as if you couldn't hear them right,
as if they were maybe calling
not from just across the water
but Timbuktu, or from the moon…

At least you can hear me, my darling,
I'm speaking so softly and clearly,
and this is a charge not a pleading.

Done

We've come to bag the evidence.
This might be the scene of a murder.
Dustsheets and silence and blame.

The flat empties its stomach into the hall.
We have given back letters and eaten our words.
You wrote off the Volvo. I gave you verrucas.

And like the window of a jeweller's after closing
the shelves in the study offer up nothing.
I slowly take the steps down one by one,

and for the first time maybe,
notice the chaos, the smouldering traffic,
the litter, bystanders, what have you

The Last Saturday in Ulster

Behind her radiator
the leather purse is caring
for the old denominations:
liverspots of giant pennies,
fifty pences thick as lenses.

A Pentecostal home outside Armagh:
antimacassars, oxygen masks,
Martha glancing towards the screen
as if checking delay and departure.

An Orange march in Antrim
will see me late arriving:
and standing out at Aldergrove
an English girl might well believe
that time is how you spend your love.

Undriven cattle graze the long acre.
Pheasants fidget and flit between townlands.
The coins were warm as new eggs
in the nest of her priestly-cool hands.

Appendix

The one we saw in the jar
had the pluperfect aura
of a worm hung in tequila,

though later, undercover, after
turning away from each other,
out of the blue, or wherever

it is that we wander in slumber,
suddenly you, or whoever *you* are
half-asleep, whisper

It was a reminder of other.

How could I not remember the summer
your vermicular organ turned fatter
turned squatter, and left you the scar

that I brush with the tip of my finger,
a doubter, before sliding the duvet over
to cover that badge of danger and care?

The curtains surface in dawn's slow exposure.
Our neighbour starts up her car and you shiver.
Hushing our avenue's branches, the wind's timbre

is pitched closer to anger than wonder.

Leon McAuley

Leon McAuley was born in Dungannon, Co. Tyrone, in 1952. He has worked as
a teacher and writer in residence in schools; he was the presenter of the Radio
Ulster book programme *You're booked* throughout its lifetime and was a regular
contributor to Radio Ulster programmes. He has edited an anthology of children's
writing, *Glistening Emeralds, Grassy Knees* and as artist-in-the-community with the
Verbal Arts Centre has collected photographs and reminiscences from a housing
estate in Derry/Londonderry entitled *The Fountain*. *Trio 4* (Blackstaff Press, 1985)
represented a selection of poetry before the publication of a single collection,
Veronica (Lagan Press, 1994).

Leon McAuley's poetry is an acute register of relationships, a barometer of
the shifting moods of love, a record of how strangely untameable the human
imagination is. Love's fragility, evolution and persistence is recorded and
celebrated in precise images and in contexts where jealousy, claustrophobia,
the limitations of subjectivity or just plain bad-timing are as likely as comfort,
certainty or synchronicity. Humour and wit are key features or vital defences
in a poetry of carefully balanced tensions. Direct, frank confrontations in poems
meet an adult demand for honest encounters of ordinary experiences of family,
home, childhood and locale; precise concrete images sit alongside an elusive, light-
footed allegiance to inner dreams and the imagination, to the rhythms and rhymes
demanded by the poem. The result is a poetry that, paradoxically, produces a
lyrical but enigmatic reality; the familiar and strange, the known and unknown,
sit alongside each other as necessary counterweights. The logic of strict form and
imaginative freedom make for other tensions in the poems; a key recurrent image,
for instance, is of claustrophobic enclosure (the Madonna in her "plastic bubble",
the oxygen tent, Houdini's handcuffs, the space capsule) from which the poem (or
its subjects) attempt escape. The poem 'Corn Circles' recasts the dilemma, a kind
of battle between revolution/youth and resignation/age, succinctly: "To dream is as
important as to know:/to love where we have been/but still to want to go."

Corn Circles

for Pauline

Who would have thought
it could have happened here -
in Broughshane, of a Sunday -
whatever it was that wrought
this ripened field of barley

to a state of such perfection?
Giotto - the artist, not the satellite -
did this sort of thing with one hand tied
behind his back.
We're not only human. We're

capable of anything we put our minds to:
the *Saturnalia of Ireland's Saturday Night.*
It's not that I don't wish or care
for scientific fact or explanation.
It's just that I'd prefer

to let my imagination
wander. To dream
is as important as to know:
to love where we've been
but still to want to go.

The Family Gathered

No, I am
finding it increasingly difficult
to picture myself,
particularly to myself,
as the young rebel
I somehow
know I am.

I have children
myself now
and lay down the law -
as if by some sudden miracle
I know the law
myself, now
I have children.

Still and all,
I'd be lying
in the face of reality
not to admit the possibility
that sooner rather than later
I'll be lying
still, and all

the family gathered
round me -
the older generation,
the increasingly younger rebels -
as you lie here tonight,
still, and round us all
the family gathered.

Jacob

The angels walk
all over me
as softly and as free
as the light
falls through my window
or the wind
blows through the trees.

Nor am I more diminished
by these gentle victories
than the singing of the wind-harp
when the wind falls to a breeze
or the wild ducks disappearing
to their northern territories.

But this wrestling with pure spirits
is a solitary kind of sin:
you're forever wrestling angels
and the angels always win.

Garlic

is white-
ness
tinged with mauve

is sacerdotal,
clothed
in stiffened silk,

and not without its sting:
Is said
to purify the blood.

In the kitchen
I sang
as I split the clove

and the kettle
was singing
on the stove

for garlic,
garlic
dry as bone

clutched tight
to emptiness -
a baby fist -

touched
like a relic
to throat and wrist

and blood-
stained
and fanged

and very much in love...

A Pair of Handcuffs

You know what it's like
when you don't want to, or haven't the time
and you say you're all tied up. That may work fine
for people like you and me. Cuts no ice with Houdini.
Without handcuffs and gag, straightjacket and chain, he
would have been lost for work, if not for words, and we
would have lost an emblem for our age.

Both artist and escapist, he turned
our claustrophobic nightmare into mime.
Dark circles round cherubic eyes,
Harry Houdini, sage enough to see
how handcuffs, by their very nature, rhyme.

Knock, Knock

Through the electronic wizardry
of a static-ridden PA
the clergy trumpet Armageddon -
this might be Judgement Day.

Weapons of mass destruction mass
on the borders of every state
and among the tawdry relic stalls,
'How's business?' 'Going great!'

My mother-in-law collects souvenirs
of the Mother-of-all-Battles
to give to her friends in Crossmaglen
to place with their goods and chattels.

Rejecting the giant rosary beads
and Bouquet of Masses forms
I choose instead, a Made-in-Taiwan
Madonna-of-All-Snowstorms,

who, trapped in her plastic bubble,
with scarcely room to sneeze,
conjures internal blizzards, like me,
with seemingly consummate ease.

Thought Bubbles

A lady in a snowstorm,
a goldfish in a bowl,
a spaceman in his helmet,
a diver in a shoal

of goldfish.
A baby in an incubator,
a pilot in a Spitfire,
your scent in an atomiser,

a saint at a country shrine
wrapped in polythene,
the man I loved in his oxygen tent,
now distant and serene.

The Chair
from Veronica

In the Queen's house
in Mount Charles

I took the chair,
you took the floor

in your burgundy
crushed-velvet flares

your platform clogs
and cheese-cloth shirt -

or was that me?
What did you wear?

Your corduroy maxi-skirt?
Were we burning joss sticks?

Playing *Horslips*?
It seems so long ago

I'm not quite sure.
I just remember

we were terribly thin
and you ate a satsuma

a thingammyjig,
a man, a mandarin.

I remember you remarked
on its dryness,

its lack of zest,
and you laid out its skin
in a circle, like the sun.
You rayed it

with burnt-out matches.
You patterned it

and played with it
in total silence

until night began to fall.
You raised your head:

'You think that you know me.
You really don't know me at all.'

Colonist

I am the shoreline: you are the sea;
I am the lock: you are the key;

I am the slate: you are the felt;
I am *Anschauung:* you are *die Welt*;

I am the mirror: you are the face;
I am the colonist: you know your place;

I am the candle: you are the flame;
I can't describe it: you are the name;

I am the short of it: you are the long;
Were I a singer, you'd be the song;

I am pure bafflement: you are pure fight,
I am blind fury: you are a sight;

I am exhausted now: switch out the light.
I am exhausted now: switch out the light.

from **Craters**

'Earth to space station. Earth to space station.
Are you receiving me? Over. Come to bed!'
The bedroom is an exact replica of the study.
Stanza upon stanza. 'This could go on all night.'
I should be so lucky! Leon! Come to bed!' *'Stanza*
from the Latin sto, starry, steady,
station - to stand.' 'Come to bed!' 'What for?
We'll only fight.' Her voice is a disembodied whisper
from the pitch-black of the stairs.
'Well then, at least let's fight.' 'Do you remember
that night in Sligo when he stared into the pitch-black
and mimed *Margaret, are you grieving?* across the theatre
staring directly at you - do you remember?'
'Yes, I remember.' 'Of course you do.
Didn't he sound precisely like a lover?'
'What does a lover sound like?' 'You remember.
Remember how the room lit up?' 'Who cares?' 'I do.'
'Just come to bed.' 'Why? Space station to earth, what for?
Are you receiving me? Are you receiving me? Over.'

Gearóid Mac Lochlainn

Gearóid Mac Lochlainn was born in 1966. He studied Scholastic Philosophy and Literature at Queen's University, Belfast. He is currently a musician with the reggae band, Bréag, and writer-in-residence in the Irish language at Queen's and the University of Ulster. His poetry publications are *Babylon Gaeilgeoir* (An Clochán, 1997) and *Na Scéalaithe* (Coiscéim, 1999); the bi-lingual selected poems *Stream of Tongues/Sruth Teangacha* (Clo iar-Chonnachta, 2002) and the volume *Rakish Paddy Blues* (open house festival.com, 2004) are accompanied by CDs.

This is poetry with great musical energy and an instinctive feel for language as music. At a literal level the poems explore the terrain of Belfast (using the wild west as a parallel) and chart shifts between the city of the Troubles and childhood and the post-ceasefire North of adulthood. The poetry also registers shifting relationships between words: the space between Irish and English, oral performance and written word, improvisation and literary tradition, the rural and urban, reality and dream, anxiety and harmony. Poems are closely allied to song and dance which shape syntax; in translations the poet hopes for tonal harmony as opposed to equivalence or, impossible, literal semantic renderings. Sean-nós, Jazz and Blues, rap, reggae and traditional music are close to the spirit of poems; the linguistically inventive (in puns, asides, in the use of Belfast idiom or satirical black humour) is also important. Inventing a macaronic or Creole tongue these poem-songs in Irish-English celebrate language as playful, non-utilitarian and non-materialistic (symbolised by Crazy Horse) and language as resistance, a record of loss - the loss of the Irish language itself. The poetry questions and celebrates translation as an ambiguous act: futile and inventive, healingly collaborative or potentially colonial, a loss of original music and gain in the creation of new poems; translation appears as both a widening of meaning and as a half-grasped joke at the expense of the monoglot. In affirming poetry as story, as well as tune or song, the poetry keeps faith with a narrative tradition that is fragile but resilient, that begins when "decades long ago./A gang of us gathered under the smashed street lamp…"

Na hEalaíontóirí

B'aistriúcháin muid,
gealacha briste ag crithlonrú
ar thonnta de bhualadh bos dorcha.

B'anáil muid, comhréir, stad,
línte scaoilte,
teanga bhláth na n-airní
ag cleitearnach go suaimhneach
idir iall oscailte an leoin
is mearbhall mire
an luascáin eitilte.

Féitheog muid,
spréite, sáite go domhain
i gclapsholas síoraí.
Lóló agus May,
Ion agus Iang.
Ár nglóir fite fuaite
i nglaise chanbháis.
Rois muid cniotáil dhubh na gcogar
sna taobhanna.

I gcaochadh na súl, tá sé imithe -
Scáth-thír, snap na gcomhlaí
Níl fágtha ach mothú de rud éigin
mar mhin sáibh,
corraíl rópaí,
scáthphictiúir thanaí
bailte is sráidbhailte
ag dul in éag
mar ghas.

The Artists

We were translations,
shattered moons shimmering
on waves of dark applause.

We were breath, syntax, pause,
lines unpegged,
the language of sloe flowers
fluttering between the lion's mouth
and the trapeze.

We were sinew
stretched and splayed
deep into endless dusk.
Lolo and May,
Yin and Yang.
We conspired with
a grey weave of canvas,
unraveled the chiaroscuro
of whisper in the aisles.

Blink and it's gone.
Shadow-land and shutter-snap.
All that's left is a hint of something,
like the feel of saw dust,
a flurry of rope,
stalk-thin silhouettes
of fading towns
and villages.

Translated by Gearóid Mac Lochlainn

Na Scéalaithe

Oíche bháistí Aoine ag deireadh Feabhra,
cluinim mionphléascáin an Playstation nua sa seomra taobh liom
ina bhfuil mo mhac is a chara greamaithe den scáileán teicnidhaite
ina lonnaíonn a chuid teicneo-laochra aeir.
Titeann suan orm.
Luím siar ag aislingiú go n-éirím as mo chorp
ar eiteoga fíneálta snáthadánacha mo chuimhne,
ar foluain mar héileacaptar arm na Breataine
thar shráideanna cúnga m'óige ar an eastát nua.

Clapsholas.
Muid inár mbaiclí, cruinn thart ar lampa sráide briste,
ag cur allais i ndiaidh cluiche *Rap-the-doors* nó *Kick-the-tin*,
ag éisteacht le traonach uaigneach ag screadach sna páirceanna
ar an taobh eile den bhóthar mór,
ag amharc aníos i ndiaidh réalta reatha nó réalta scuaibe
a d'imeodh as radharc chomh gasta
le samhraí m'óige is an traonach glórach féin.

Anseo faoin lampa briste a shuigh muid -
finscéalaithe an eastáit tithíochta
lenár scéalta leathfhíor, leathchumtha - ár gcuid scéalta cogaidh.
Bhí a fhois againn fiú ansin
go raibh gunnaí curtha faoin chosán,
fite i measc na gcáblaí aibhléise.
Anseo a phléigh muid an t-óglach síoraí
in áiléar tí feirme folamh ar imeall an eastáit,
ag déanamh féasta ar luchóga móra is uibheacha dreoilín,
nó ina luí mar mharbhán, curtha le trí lá
i gcónra urlár adhmaid comharsan ciúine,
gan bhíog as.
Iógaí poblachtach.

The Storytellers
28 February 1998

The last Friday in February: it's pouring rain outside,
and I'm getting the flak from the Playstation in the next room
where my son and his mate are glued to the screenful
of techno-heroes locked in technicoloured combat.
I must have dozed off, or drifted out of my body
to hover like a British army helicopter
on the viewless wings of poesy
above the planned streets of the new estate.

It's dusk. It's decades long ago.
A gang of us have gathered under the smashed street-lamp,
breathless after playing Rap-the doors, or Kick-the tin,
ears pricked to the lonesome call of a freight-train
rumbling through the darkened fields beyond the motorway:
a noise which fades as instantly as those stars
we watched fall to earth so many years ago.

Hunkered under the broken lamp,
we were masters of the universe of story,
the legendary half-truths of the war years.
We were clued up to the guns stashed under paving-stones,
clips of bullets sleeved between electric cables.
Here we swore eternal comradeship,
envisaging the empty hay-loft on the frontier of the new estate
where we'd scavenge for rats and wrens' eggs;
or stretch out like corpses
under a neighbour's floorboards for three days,
stiff as boards -
birth-pangs of the revolution.

Anseo, m'anáil íslithe
a chuala mé faoin scuadaí, seacht mbliana déag d'aois,
a chaill cos ag tabhairt cic do channa folamh Coca Cola
inar cuireadh cnaipe bídeach Semtex.
An para a chaill a phoill sróine
ag mothú lusa chromchinn i bPáirc na bhFál.
Scéal faoin nóíbhíseach
a phléasc é féin ina mhíle píosa thíos ag na dugaí
is a bhí ite suas go hiomlán ag colmáin sráide ocracha
is faoileáin shantacha nár fhág lorg ná rian
do na póilíní is a gcuid bleachtairí.

Pléascann m'óige ionam nuair a chuimhním
ar na poill philéar úra sna brící meirgrua
inar shleamhnaigh muid méara faiteacha,
mar a dhéanfaí ar thaisí naofa
as a dtiocfadh ádh is dea-rudaí dúinn,
is an t-am ar tháinig muid ar raidhfil is gránáid
clúdaithe i saicéadach glas, i bhfolach sna tithe leath-thógtha
ina ndearna muid base nuair a bhí sé ag cur
do mhalartú mirlíní is piléir phlaisteacha.
Amanna bhí iontais le feiceáil,
mar an hata círéibe le cealtair
Is cumhdach piostail a shábháil na deartháireacha Magee
ó jíp a tiontaíodh bun os cionn
ag cath reatha i lár na hoíche.

Shíl muid go raibh muid saor
mar Khunta Kinte agus Chicken George,
soar mar Kung Fú Cain na feadóige, ag síorshiúl
dhromchla an domhain ghránna, gan eagla.
Soar mar Lin Chung as Liang Shan Po
is lean muid a lorg go mórshúileach
mar scata moncaithe nite le málaí milseán
os comhair doras draíochta na teilifíse.

Níos moille
fuair muid laochra níos cóngaraí don bhaile,

I held my breath
as I heard the one about the seventeen-year-old Brit
whose leg was blown off when he happened to kick
a pellet-of-Semtex-loaded empty Coke tin.
The para who got an extra hole in his nose
from sniffing coke in the Falls Park.
The rookie volunteer who blew himself to smithereens
down by the docks.
Pickings for the gulls and pigeons:
not a scrap left for Forensics.

Riot after riot,
years of brick walls riddled with fresh bullet-holes
which we prodded with our fingertips
for good luck, like doubting Thomases, wanting to believe.
Swapping marbles and plastic bullets on rainy days at base.
Magnificent trophies,
like the riot helmet and face-shield,
salvaged by the two Magees
from a jeep capsized in an early morning ambush.

We thought we were free,
like Kunta Kinte and Chicken George
free as cool-fluting Kung Fu Cain
walking the back of the world with no fear,
free as Lin Chung from Liang Shan Po,
dogging his footsteps
like a troop of monkeys munching KP nuts
before the magic portal of the TV.

Before long
we found more down-home heroes.

muid ag malartú
suaitheantas dubh is bán
le haghaidheanna doiléire na stailceoirí ocrais orthu.
Chuir muid de ghlanmheabhair ár dtáblaí iarscoile -

Bobby Sands, May 5, 66 days
Francis Hughes, May 12, 61 days
Raymond McCresh, May 19, 61 days...

San oíche is mé faoi na braillíní sa dorchadas,
ag éisteacht le fuaimeanna fadálacha diamhra na sráide
thiontaíodh *tiltswitch* beag ionam
gur shamhlaigh mé íobairtí móra
a dhéanfainn féin do mhuintir Éireann.
Sa nanashoicind idir chodladh is dúiseacht
gheobhainn spléachín den phoblacht órga
mhistéireach le teacht,
sula dtagadh suan orm -

Thomas Mc Elwee, Aug 8
Mickey Devine, Aug 20...

Ar maidin bhíodh na sráideanna líonta lán
le *halfers* agus *hickers*, buidéil bhriste, tinte beaga,
púcaí toite liatha, is scéalta, finscéalta,
ráflaí laochra sráide, luaithríona, cumhracht pheitril is rubar dóite
is cnámharlaigh bhusanna Uladh, dóite amach,
ina luí mar chorpáin lofa eilifintí brónacha
a chuaigh ar strae san oíche ar na bóithre dorcha.

Ba leanaí cogaidh muid,
páistí a thuig greann na círéibe,
cumhachtaí draíochta piléar,
castachtaí cruálacha buamaí.
Bhíodh ár mbrionglóidí trom le *binlids* is *barricades*
is taipéis laethanta órga grian-nite samhraidh
fite le *tripwires* na samhlaíochta.

We swapped black and white badges
Xeroxed with the stark faces of the men on hunger-strike.
We'd recite them like our times tables:

Bobby Sands, May 5, 66 days
Francis Hughes, May 12, 61 days
Raymond Mc Cresh, May 19, 61 days...

Huddled under my blanket in the dead of night,
I'd tune my ears to the whirrs and clicks of the street,
and feel a little tilt-switch in me turn me on
to dreams of sacrifice for Ireland.
In that twilight zone, for one split chink of time,
I'd glimpse the imminent republic in all its majesty
before sleep wiped it out...

Thomas Mc Elwee, August 8
Mickey Devine, August 20...

Come dawn, the streets would be littered
with halfers, broken bottles, tongues of flame
smouldering among the rubble,
muttering of ruins, ashes, rumours, epic escapades,
the whiff of petrol and rubber,
the twisted skeletons of Ulsterbuses
slumped like burned-out mammoths.

We were war urchins,
wise kids, well versed in riotous behaviour.
We knew the amulet powers of the bullet,
the cruel complexion of the bomb.
Our dreams were fraught with barricades and binlids,
the golden tapestry of burning summer days
wrought with the glittering tripwires
of imagination.

Translated by Ciaran Carson

Teanga Eile

Mise an teanga
i mála an fhuadaitheora,
liopaí fuaite le snáthaid,
cosa ag ciceáil.

Mise an teanga
sínte ar bhord an bhúistéara
in oifigí rialtais, géaga ceangailte,
corp briste brúite
curtha faoi chlocha
ar chúl claí
roimh bhreacadh an lae.

Mise an teanga
a fhilleann san oíche, ceolta sí, Micí Mi-ádh.
Snámhaim trí na cáblaí aibhléise,
ceolaim os íseal
i bhfiliméad an bholgáin ar do thábla.
Eitlím trí na pasáistí dúdhorcha rúnda
faoin chathair bhriste.

Mise an teanga a sheachnaíonn tú
ar na bóithre dorcha,
i dtábhairní. Croí dubh.
Fanaim ort faoi lampa sráide buí
ag an choirnéal.
Leanaim do lorg mar leannán diúltaithe.

Mise an teanga a thostaigh tú.
Ortha mé,
i bpóca dubh an fhile choirr
i muinín déirce.

Second Tongue

I am the tongue
in the kidnapper's sack
lips stitched, feet flailing.
I am the tongue
bound on the butcher's block
in government offices,
a battered, broken corpse
ditched at dawn.
I am the tongue
who comes in the night.
I am jinx
swimming through flex
and electricity cables.
I sing softly in the element of the bulb
on your table.
I am Johnny Dark, Creole.
I wing through secret pitch-black passageways
beneath the broken city.
I am the tongue
you shun on dark roads, in pubs.
I am hoodoo
waiting for you on the corner
under the yellow street lamp,
stalking you like a jilted John.
I am the tongue
you silenced. I am patois.
I am mumbo-jumbo, juju,
a mojo of words
in the back pocket
of the weirdo poet
busking for bursaries.

Translated by Séamus Mac Annaidh and Gearóid Mac Lochlainn

Ag an Tábla

Ní féidir éisteacht leis an ghlór seo níos mó,
druilire searbh focal é a thollann tríom,
mar fhuaim an mheaisín níocháin ar casadh.
Croitheann sé na néaróga, gur mhian liom rith
is míle doras druidte is dorchlaí a chur idir mé is an t-inneall mire
a chuireann na cupáin ar crith ar an tseilf.
Nó mar shíorscread an *hoover* ag fórsáil a mhuiníl chaoil isteach
sa dorchadas faoin seantolg briste,
a ghaosán géar a shá sna cúinní ciúine dorcha.
Ní féidir pioc den bhéile a ithe
is na focail faobhair seo ag polladh mo chinn,
ag stolladh is ag sracadh mo chuid smaointe
mar a bheadh mo chloigeann curtha tríd an *blender* leictreach
is m'intinn steallta mar shú talún brúite
thar bhabhla plaisteach an *liquidizer*.

Tá mo chéachta oscailte
ach ní féidir dada a mhothú.
Ní chluinim fiú na páistí ag caoineadh thuas staighre níos mó.
Táim dall is bodhar.
Ní mhothaím ach an scian seo teannta i mo lámh,
ba mhian liom í a shá is a shá arís go díoltasach,
isteach i gcroí an ghlóir sin,
é a stróiceadh is a ghearradh as a chéile;
go gcruthóinn tost iomlán.
Tost naofa fuildorcha.

At the Table

That's it. I can't take any more.
The words are an electric drill,
or a washing machine going through the spin cycle.
It sets my teeth on edge.
Stash the mad gadget behind locked doors!
I can't, it's a hoover whining and probing its trunk
into the dark beneath the broken sofa.
I can't eat a pick.
My head's been bored through and through.
They're blending my brains in a Magimix.
They're processing my mind like soup.

The wounds are still raw,
but I can hear fuck-all.
The kids are crying upstairs - so what?
I've just gone deaf. Gone blind too.
All I know is the kitchen knife in my fist,
which I'll stick and stick again into
the throbbing heart of the squawking head
till it's been ripped apart for good.
Then I'll have made proper peace.
Dark holy bloody peace.

Translated by Ciaran Carson

Deireadh Cóisire

Coinnle múchta,
feadóg faoi shuan,
gloine diúgtha,
maindilín is fidil i leaba a mbosca,
spalpadh cainte scaipthe.

Draíocht ag síothlú
as an oíche.

Ach éist.
Focail athmhúscailte.
Peann ag damhsa.

When the Session's Over

Candle snuffed
whistle blown
glass drained
talk piped down
tunes reeled in.

Magic seeps from the night.

But listen.
Words awake.
Line dancing.

Translated by Gearóid Mac Lochlainn
and Rónán Ó Snodaigh

Barraíocht
do Chaoimhín Mac Giolla Chatháin

Tá mé tinn
Barraíocht toitíní i mo bhosca ceoil
Barraíocht beorach i mo sconna óir
Barraíocht pinginí i mo phócaí folmha
Barraíocht pócaí i mo bhríste briste
Tá barraíocht de bharraíocht ina bharraíocht dom
Tá mo thine trí thine is tá mé tinn

Tá mé tinn
Barraíocht gréine i mo choillín geal
Barraíocht déithe i mo chailís
Barraíocht síochána i mo chupán déirce
Barraíocht cuileog thar mo bhod

Barraíocht nóiníní i mo thrilse
Barraíocht fidleacha i mo chófra
Barraíocht daoine i mo chistin fhuar fholamh
Barraíocht leac oighir i mo dheoch dhúr
Tá barraíocht de bharraíocht ina bharraíocht dom
Tá mo thine trí thine is tá mé tinn

Tá mé tinn
Barraíocht fuisce i mo chupán caife
Barraíocht uisce i mo thobar beannaithe
Barraíocht féir i mo chluain mhór
Barraíocht fearthainne I mo gheimhreadh

Barraíocht striapach ar mo shráid
Barraíocht oícheanta i lár mo mhíosa
Barraíocht sú i ngas mo phinn
Barraíocht goirm i mo spéir dhubh

Too Much

I'm sick
Too many joints in my music box
Too much black beer in my golden tap
Too many pennies in my pockets
Too many pockets in my broke-down-pants
My fire is on fire and I'm sick

I'm sick
Too much sunshine in my weird wood
Too many gods in my chalice
Too much peace in my begging cup
Too many flies on my piece

Too many daisies in my dreadlocks
Too many fiddlers in my cupboard
Too many people's come-on-in my kitchen
Too much ice in my dour dram
My fire is on fire and I'm sick

I'm sick
Too much Powers in my coffee cup
Too much water in my holy well
Too much hay in my high meadow
Too much rain in my winter

Too many whores on my street
Too many dark nights in the middle of my month
Too much ink in my pen
Too many blues in my black skies

Barraíocht buairimh i mo leaba lom
Barraíocht luchóg ag ithe mo chuid cáise
Barraíocht piollaí faoi mo philiúr
Tá barraíocht de bharraíocht ina bharraíocht domh
Tá mo thine trí thine is tá mé tinn
Tá mé tinn
Barraíocht dathanna i mo thuar ceatha casta
Barraíocht *hippy* ag mo chóisir
Barraíocht piléar i m'fhobhríste
Barraíocht dánta i mo bhabhla leithris
Barraíocht léinn is barraíocht crá
Barraíocht bréag i mo litreacha grá

Barraíocht Búda faoi mo chrann figí
Barraíocht Craoisneá ag an bhord dinnéir
Barraíocht de bharraíocht ina bharraíocht dom
Tá mo thine trí thine is tá mé tinn

Tá mé tinn
Tá mé tinn, a chairde, tá mé tinn.

Too much worry in my bare bed
Too many mice at my cheese
Too many pills under my pillow
Too much of a muchness is too much for me
My fire is on fire and I'm sick

I'm sick
Too many colours in my black rainbow
Too many hippies at my party
Too many bullets in my trunks
Too many poems in my toilet bowl
Too much learning and too much heartache
Too many lies in my love letters

Too many Buddhas under my fig tree
Too much Krishna at my table
Too much of a muchness is too much for me
My fire is on fire and I'm sick.

I'm sick people, say sick.

Translated by Gearóid Mac Lochlainn

Crazy Horse ag Damhsa

Since the time of his youth Crazy Horse had known that the world men lived in
was only a shadow of the real world. To get to the real world, he had to dream,
and when he was in the real world everything seemed to float or dance… No
photograph of Crazy Horse has ever been authenticated
    - Dee Brown

Grian ag dul faoi,
ag ghaoth ina buile,
fuil ag deargadh an locha,
géaga linbh crochta ar chrann
Tá Crazy Horse ag damhsa.

Tormán na gcos
ag buaireamh na marbh
lúth a choirp ag suaitheadh an aeir.

Uaill chaointe,
mac tíre ag fánaíocht
i mbrionglóidí na hoíche,
osna ó bhroinn an domhain,
Crazy Horse ag damhsa thar tine.

Dordán cicada,
monabhar uisce,
brioscarnach lasracha
mar thionlacan.

I siosarnach na nduilleog
cluintear glórtha na sinsear,
tá Crazy Horse ag damhsa
is ní féider cime grianghraif
a dhéanamh de.

Le titim na gealaí
scaoiltear aislingí;
athbheirtear Crazy Horse arís.

Crazy Horse Dancing

Sun, he go down
wind, he go crazy
lake, all blood
child, hang from tree
Crazy Horse, he dance

his feet stir the dead
slim limbs
put air in tizzy

wail and howl
wandering wolf
dreams of night
sigh from womb of world

Crazy Horse, he dance with fire
cicada, he drone
water, he murmur
flame, he crackle
all join in

leaves whisper
songs of the living-dead

Crazy Horse, he dance
but not for eye

moon, he go down
vision comes up

Crazy Horse,
he born again
man

Translated by Gabriel Rosenstock

Amhrán Chrazy Horse

Cé hé Crazy Horse, cé hé?
Cuir ceist ar na bláthanna.

Cé hé Crazy Horse, cé hé?
Cuir ceist ar na scáthanna.

Cé hé Crazy Horse, cé hé?
Cuir ceist ar na pháiste.

Cé hé Crazy Horse, cé hé?
Cuir ceist ar an ghealach.

Cé hé Crazy Horse, cé hé?
Cuir ceist ar an ghrian.

Cé hé Crazy Horse, cé hé?
Cuir ceist ar do chroíse.

Cé hé Crazy Horse, cé hé?
Féach taobh istigh.

Féach é ag damhsa.

Crazy Horse Sings

Crazy Horse? Who he, Crazy Horse?
go ask flower

Crazy Horse? Who he, Crazy Horse?
go ask shadow

Crazy Horse? Who he, Crazy Horse?
go ask child

Crazy Horse? Who he, Crazy Horse?
go ask moon

Crazy Horse? Who he, Crazy Horse?
go ask sun

Crazy Horse? Who he, Crazy Horse?
go ask heart

Crazy Horse? Who he, Crazy Horse?
look in

See, he dance.

Translated by Gabriel Rosenstock

Do William Kennedy
agus do Brian Vallely

The only thing I ask of God now is health, for as to fortune, He has given me an exhaustless one in my workshop. The blind ones in this world are not they who cannot see the sun, but they who cannot see duty…
   - William Kennedy

Is ó am go ham
Is na poirt séidte
Is clapsholas na séise ag cuisliú ionat
Ag síothlú uait
Is scáthanna dorcha codlata ag druidim leat
Ag tuirlingt tharat, mar fhéileacáin oíche
Seans, go mbraithfidh tú as an nua
Trí shúile an phíobaire dhaill
Ribíní rúnda ríleanna reatha
Breachta le ruaille buaille dathanna
Castaí is lúba órga crónán cornphíopa
Scrabhadh, scríobh
Is peannaireacht aeir na fidile
Barraí ildaite ag doirteadh go fras
Ina bhfoinsí geala fonn
Liosanna seanda fuaime
Guthanna giúiseanna
Is spéirmhná caointe
Ag scaipeadh soilse ceoil is cantaireachta
Ar an bhóthar romhat…
Is ansin, suaimhneach ciúin,
Is codladh sámh.

To William Kennedy
and to Brian Vallely

And sometimes
In the afterglow of a session
As the chiaroscuro of sleep seeps over you
You may begin to see anew
As if through the hollow eyes of William Kennedy
Ribbons ripples and twists of dappled reels
Twirls of treble and bass
The flourish and scroll of jigs
Aural scribbles
The scratch and scrawl of fiddles
Streaming bars and beams of airs
Lambent haloes of hum
The flickering lustre of sonic loops
Purred spangles of decibel
Vibrations
The coiled spectres of sound
That light the way
Then sleep
Sound asleep

Johnny Doran

do Aoibh agus James

Sea mhaise, dá mbeadh mileoidean agamsa
Ní bheadh Críost gan cheol anocht
         -Eoghan Ó Tuairisc, Oíche Nollag

Is sheinnfinn ceol cuisle duit
Ceolta gaoithe lán calláin duit
Ceol cúlstaighre chiorclaigh duit
Dhéanfainn duit ceol

Is sheinnfinn ceol cistí duit
Ceol duillí darach dorcha duit
Ceol cladaigh ceol ceonna
Dhéanfainn duit ceol

Is murar leor é sin
Bhuel is cuma liomalinn
Ní bheidh deireadh leis an cheol seo go deo

Is sheinnfinn ceolta sí duit
Ceol cuisleannach ciúin duit
Ceol casúir ceol bóthair
Is dhéanfainn duit ceol

Ceol cúlchistine ceolmhaire
Is cairde go leor ann
Iad taobh leis an tine
Ag síorbhualadh ceoil

Is murar leor é sin
Bíodh sé go breá binnilinn
Is iomlán gealaí ag gáirí

Johnny Doran
for the Doran family

Johnny played staccato vibrato legato
Rubato shapes of open streets
An' Rakish Paddy blues

An' Johnny played on the beat off the beat of the beat
Regulator syncopated
Rakish Paddy blues

An' Johnny played waterfalls fox chase music halls
Hurley sticks an' horse fairs
Rakish Paddy blues

An' churring tunes of crescent moons
An' buttercups of horses shoes
An' chimin' bells of bluebell blues
He brings the harvest home

An' Johnny played the fancy trill street corner colour spill
Open tight an' free style
Rakish Paddy blues

An' Johnny played short rolls long rolls double rolls
Tipping on the same note
Rakish Paddy blues

An' Johnny shaped silver keys
On metal rimmed wagon wheels
Hammer tapped the anvil
Rakish Paddy blues

Is sheinnfinn ceol meidhreach malartach mealltach
Tintreach is toirneach
Is dhéanfainn duit ceol

Comhshondas comhshondach
Le macallaí sna hallaí
Is líonfainn duit málaí
De cheathanna ceoil

Is murar leor é sin
Sure is cuma liomalinn
Beidh an fíor-rud againn ar ball

An' delight the night with starbright pipes
An' wheels that roll through wreaths of road
An' chained with daisies to 'is chanter
He brings the harvest home

An' Johnny played North Clare, cattle markets, Eyre Square
Stomp an' champ of dappled mares
An' Rakish Paddy blues

An' Johnny played open roads minor roads cross roads
Dawn chorus campfires
An' Rakish Paddy blues

An' Johnny sang duende the nuances and nooks
Travelling the inner routes
Of Rakish Paddy blues

An' Coppers an' Brass an' The Fermoy Lassies
The Bunch of Keys an' journeywork
An' churnin' breeze into changeling airs
He brings the harvest home

Nigel McLoughlin

Nigel McLoughlin was born in Enniskillen in 1968. He holds an M.A. and Ph.D. in Creative Writing from Lancaster University and has lectured in Traditions at The Poets' House in County Donegal (2000 - 2004). He currently lives in Gloucester where he is Field Chair in Creative Writing at the University of Gloucestershire. McLoughlin has also co-edited an anthology of new Irish poets, *Breaking the Skin* (Black Mountain Press, 2002); his three collections of poetry are entitled *At the Waters' Clearing* (Flambard/Black Mountain Press, 2001), *Songs for No Voices* (Lagan Press, 2004) and *Blood* (bluechrome, 2005).

The North of Ireland, from the urban north-east and Belfast to the west of Donegal and Fermanagh, are key locations in Nigel McLoughlin's poetry. The poetry bears witness to historical pressures or fissures: the long history of violence in the North, in particular, and Ireland, in general; the suppression of traditions such as the Irish language; the sense of inner exile or literal, historic exile via emigration that is particularly, acutely, felt in the border county of Donegal. The poetry also seeks (with a balance of toughness and tenderness) through formal, but varied, verse forms to rebuild fragile connections between people, landscape and language. In so doing the poetry adopts, adapts and fuses the language of contemporary people (often on the fringe of society) and the language of poetic tradition to restore a sense of language itself as primary or living - as the very means by which we name, celebrate, and historically (even tenuously) exist in the world.

Urban Myth

It started surreptitiously
to appear, spray-painted,
on fences, walls, flagstones:
MENTOL + GAIL
in black block letters.
It grew more daring,
running from the sides of trains;
jumping from the tops of bridges.

Legends started, spread,
of mad bikers and beautiful
girls in leather dangling
from the undersides of tunnels.
It was everywhere for a while;
on roundabouts; on the backs
of busses and, some say, shaved
on a monkey's arse in Belfast Zoo.

I used to wonder if they
settled down to kids,
a mortgage maybe or
perhaps a career with
Saatchi or the circus.
Then I saw a skinny
skinhead spraying on
the wall at Queen's:

MENTOL + GAIL
in black block letters.
I asked if he was Mentol
(or Gail perhaps)
and he said, 'No, but
my mate is Mentol,
and anyway, Mentol
would have writ it,
if he'd been here.

Belfast

The stroke of a clock on the still air
and the tolling of a bell over water.
These are simple, lonely sounds,
the sounds of a city sleeping.
And each dark silence concentrates
the shape-shifting shadows on the moon.
Consecrates the night; consummates
the concrete's love of moonlight.

A slow dawn mist falls from the Cavehill,
softly eddies through streets, curls
around houses, makes myths of murals,
settles beneath flags.
And this is a city of many flags.
But today it will wake
to its only common colour.

The slow Lagan weaves below
like a murky dream, black beneath
and white above, it mingles all
our necessary shades of grey.
The river mist is rolling, birthing
a familiar landscape in something
less than stone, something more
than air. It is our dreams almost
forming, hesitant as a sleeper waking.

Stones

Passing Milltown on the last bus home,
the gravestones flicker-flame,
flare into life, just for seconds,
as if to say…
Remember how we buried truth
under martyrs, under blame;
when God was which and who,
how we poured blood for pronouns.

The lights of The Maze play in lines,
dancing chains around the gaol.
our dead rhetoric returns,
in sentences, parsed with guns.
it echoes off walls…

Haunting our silences, in these places
where those we've shut up, put
under stones, form monuments
in years, in tears, in flesh
bagged by the hundredweight.

Opus to the Manifest

I will write a stone book, a weight
to break the entropy of silence;
use a quote from *Das Kapital*
to seal my head, like a draught excluder,

erect no entry signs to the winds of change.
I will look at the world through a Moorish window
see Leopold of Austria in his last waltz,

whip it up in a mix of words and put it down
in writing. I will taste nothing. I will be tasteless.

I will sign my life away in lawsuits,
live and die an opulent graveyard of words,
drag the living shards of thought to the dark.

I will offer a dead man's manifesto:
A magnum opus of nonsense.

I will offer Art.

Forty Shades of Fuchsia

I could show you three pictures from an old man's head.
I could show you that they lasted him a lifetime.
I could show you the last tree on an island
and the men breaking their boats to bury their dead.
I could show you a sky at evening.
I could show you forty shades of fuchsia.

I could show you bodies wasting into long shadows.
I could show you men dropping where they worked.
I could show you the road to nowhere
and where they say there is hungry grass.
I could show you a field of wild flowers.
I could show you forty shades of fuchsia.

I could show you a son standing over his father.
I could show you the grip slackening on his arm.
I could show you the plea in his eyes at his last words:
'Ná bí ag briseadh baidí ar bith domsa.'
I could show you a host of boats at sail.
I could show you forty shades of fuchsia.

Voodoo

Once, I murdered him,
the man who was my double;
I drank until his liver burst,
smoked until his lungs gave out,
left every woman he ever loved.
It broke his heart in the end,
left him suicidal, killed him.
But I emerged laughing
from the wreckage of his years
and now I see, smiling
in the mirror of his cold eyes,
cold eyes.

Cattle Shed

The cattle lowed their way between the stones
of this old shed where they were herded daily
from grass to gate, until the day he fell dead
between two horses pulling a rusty thresher
up the field. Neighbours lifted him, carried him
inside and laid him out across the kitchen table.

That was forty years ago and grass grows high
around the shed. Stones have tumbled from
the roofbar, scattered to the ground and still
cattle nose around while a stranger tends the land.
The grass, the field have gathered his grave in
and death has held him tight in open hands.

Crows

Glaucous ruptures of air
turn impossibly on updrafts,
skim imminent ground.

The unlucky plummet,
become a bolus of feather
and bone, grow maggoty with life.

Tragedy is beautiful
from the outside.
Death is sweet
as silence in the throat.

The Book of Invasions

I have come here in winter
to watch darkness creep over Muckish
like an invader from the north

to watch the fire thole in stone
at the stroop of two hills
I have come here in winter

to hear the whispered notes of a white
melody strange from the stream's bed
like an invader from the north

to hear it echo, rise and dance
through rocks at the water's fall
I have come here in winter

to take the wordless air and fill it
with a populace of new language
like an invader from the north

to plunder a landscape for a refuge
to take possession and find belonging
I have come here in winter
like an invader from the north

A Chinese Woodcut

Wood and metal in the eye mock
stone and earth on the slow drive
through a gap in Donegal where
the sun is molten in the stroop
of mountains and the lake seems
to gleam and tarnish like sodium
cut and cut by a pocket-knife wind.
The trees stand rigid as scuts
of pig-iron out on the corroded
copper headland and gorse is brass
on the mahogany mountain.

I am following a man I hardly knew,
being driven to his wake thinking,
in his blind eye, which of the two is alien:
to know that in a foreigner's eye everything
can be seen in terms of metal and wood
or to realise that the day after you die
a stranger sees why the cranes fly west.

Sinéad Morrissey

Sinéad Morrissey was born in Portadown in 1972 and read English and German at Trinity College, Dublin. She has lived and worked in New Zealand and Japan and is currently writer in residence at Queen's University, Belfast. Her volumes of poetry are entitled *There Was Fire in Vancouver* (Carcanet, 1996), *Between Here and There* (Carcanet, 2002), and *The State of the Prisons* (Carcanet, 2005).

Sinéad Morrissey's poetry covers diverse territory, both literally and thematically. Poems range in locale from Japan, North America and Canada to the Antipodes and Ireland; thematically the poems explore a geography of the heart as a more loosely tied parcel than we suspect. In dealing with both literal and spiritual geographies poems unsettle us with vivid imagery and a condensed, wry wit in which the poet offers at least "two thinks at one time". 'In Belfast', for instance, reveals the way in which both travel and distance, followed by return, can produce an ambiguous response to home; dispassionate objectivity and near-sighted entanglement co-exist. 'Clothes' both agrees and disagrees with the idea that there is "more enterprise in walking naked". 'Sea Stones' and 'Stitches', respectively, reveal a complex sense of the way in which, within one heart, both healing and wounds or jealousy and love can simultaneously coexist. Poems are laced with rich, inextricable ambiguities and achieve a wide tonal range. The music in the poetry is unmistakeable too: there is the delicate undertow of a syllabic music in singing lines shaped by traditional forms at one moment, a direct conversational idiom and free verse at the next - and the co-mingling of both. In poems like 'The Juggler' or 'Jo Gravis in his Metal Garden' both poet and outsider artist become complicit in human sympathy and art making so that art emerges essentially as an act of faith in a secular age. "With all the improbables cajoled/Into truth, we are not as far out/From faith as we were".

If Words

If words became things
I'd watch a stream of unfortunates
Fall from the mouth -

Harlequin, leather,
Worn shoes and a megaphone
Blasting the second-hand
Book of the self; animal masks,
Nitrate, and all the small-minded
Weapons of fear - double-edged
Penknives, the hypodermic,
The wasp -

They spill like sewage and dismay.
I dream of the mouth as a nest
Giving flight to

Lilies, windows,
Gold letters and chimes,
Witch-hazel, a lighthouse,
An oak beam, a warm sea
And a bright white body
In the act
Of forgetting itself -
Shuddering with love.

Clothes

Once they come undone, there's no stopping the undoing
Of all that keeps us us and not we.
From a room full of history and underwear
I throw out my diary and walk naked.

Until we're talking of weather again,
Contact shrunk back to wherever it sprang from.
I'm begging for it all, coat, hats, gloves, scarf -
Shoes shod in iron, and a waterproof.

The Juggler

He must have practised for hours
Between the bins and mattresses
Of a rented back yard
To dance the seven painted skittles
Off his fingers like that.
He has the game whittled

To art. God knows what
Anachronism he took up before,
Using medieval skills to stop
Time: he puts the clock back
Nine hundred years
With this side-show for a quack

Or diversion for a king.
Still, or because of the drain
Of things modern, we ring
Him with faces. He knows
How we anticipate failure
And that what he owes

His audience is a defiance
Of breakdown. We watch as his magic
Catches the radiance
Of a spinning blue arc, brought
Slowly to a standstill. Natural begrudgers,
We are nevertheless caught

By the weightlessness, the controlled
Mechanics of air

With all the improbables cajoled
Into truth, we are not as far out
From faith as we were.

In Belfast

I

Here the seagulls stay in off the Lough all day.
Victoria Regina steering the ship of the City Hall
in this the first and last of her intense provinces,
a ballast of copper and gravitas.

The inhaling shop-fronts exhale the length
and breadth of Royal Avenue, pause,
inhale again. The city is making money
on a weather-mangled Tuesday.

While the house for the Transport Workers' Union
fights the weight of the sky and manages
to stay up, under the Albert Bridge the river
is simmering at low tide and sheeted with silt.

II

I have returned after ten years to a corner
and tell myself it is as real to sleep here
as the twenty other corners I have slept in.
More real, even, with this history's dent and fracture

splitting the atmosphere. And what I have been given
is a delicate unravelling of wishes
that leaves the future unspoken and the past
unencountered and unaccounted for.

The city weaves itself so intimately
it is hard to see, despite the tenacity of the river
and the iron sky; and in its downpour and its vapour I am
as much at home here as I will ever be.

Sea Stones

It is exactly a year today since you slapped me in public.
I took it standing up. You claimed I just ignored it,
that I pretended to be hooked on the dumb-show of a sunset,
splashing, a mile off. Too hooked to register
the sting of your ring finger
as it caught on my mouth and brought my skin with it.

All the next day I rolled with a migraine
down a merciless gallery that was mercifully without sun.
Sloshed tea in the saucer when your name came up.
I couldn't stop the cup of my hurt
flowing over and over until I saw there was no end of it
and only an end to me. How promiscuous pain can be.

He gave me roses. The surprise of butterflies caged in the palms.
And sea stones with tracings of juvenile kisses, scented with risk.
I wrapped them in black at the back of a bottom drawer,
hidden in underwear. The truth - that you never were so vivid
or so huge as the second the street turned towards us
in shock - got dropped between us like a fallen match.

You turned away as the sun disappeared like a ship. And I,
suddenly wanting to be struck again, to keep the fire of your anger lit,
I bit my lip.

& Forgive Us Our Trespasses

Of which the first is love. The sad, unrepeatable fact
that the loves we shouldn't foster burrow faster and linger longer
than sanctioned kinds can. Loves that thrive on absence, on lack
of return, or worse, on harm, are unkillable, Father.
They do not die in us. And you know how we've tried.
Loves nursed, inexplicably, on thoughts of sex,
a return to touched places, a backwards glance, a sigh -
they come back like the tide. They are with us at the terminus
when cancer catches us. They have never been away.
Forgive us the people we love - their dragnet influence.
Those disallowed to us, those who frighten us, those who stay
on uninvited in our lives and every night revisit us.
Accept from us the inappropriate
by which our dreams and daily scenes stay separate.

Stitches

There has been extravagance in speech
and every spilled, exploded word has been a stitch
in a blanket made for an imaginary baby.
The words went south where the sun was, but stayed hungry.

A name came in the third month. A face followed.
A hair type, a footprint, but the stitches showed.
Imagination's cloth too coarsely woven
for life to catch and cover stitching over.

And then blood. Inevitable, true.
Simple and strong enough to cut all falsehood through.
Later the screen said darkness - no spine, no heart.
And the stitches came apart.

Jo Gravis in His Metal Garden

Our Lady of Guadalupe appeared to a humble Indian Juan Diego,
and told him to build a church on the Tepayac Hill
but unless he could bring proof the Bishop would not believe Juan Diego
when Juan Diego told Our Lady of Guadalupe
she asked him to hold out his Tilma and there on a cold winter's day
she filled it with the roses of summer
then the Bishop believed Juan Diego and so a beautiful church
was built on Tepayac Hill
it is the most revered place of worship in Mexico
            - from the wall of a church in Tucson, Arizona

From the window of the midnight-bound Vegas plane
Tucson flares in the desert - a cactus pricked by rain;
lit houses, lit highways and floodlit swimming pools -
a stunned bird in a basin, spreading its wings to cool.
The gaudiness of Winterhaven is visible from air

in the aftermath of Christmas. Down in the dazzle somewhere
Jo Gravis is sleeping in his metal garden. It took a year
of free time strung like stepping stones from hour to hour
to finally clear his yard of rocks and the herbs he grew
as a solitary failed commercial venture - ginseng and feverfew.
Each hour of work an island. As though delivering his heart
from alcohol, he struck down to the bedrock of a humble start
and stood there a long time, exposed and rarified. At first,
he simply let the pictures come, withstood the thirst
and suffered the parade of soldiers, beggars, widows, orphans,
owls without trees and waterless swans and dolphins
until a gate latched in his mind and he had them forever.
He knew then he could commit them to metal to challenge the weather
and started to build. Metal the medium and metal the message,
he turned trolleys into children, knives into rose petals
from the pockets of Juan Diego, miraculous, crimson
a velvet gift of proof from a virgin in a vision
hardened against the sun. He peeled flesh back from the bone
and fooled no one. When his women with aerial hair were done
his kettle-headed men stood guard against them by a river
of headlights and bicycle wheels. Such honesty in silver
puts constancy in a peeled hand of wires against the sky
and hope in a speechless sort of prophecy -
a teddy bear bound with twine to an orange tree,
its eyes replaced with pearls. With all of these images
hard and permanent and real and safe in cages
Jo Gravis sensed a sweet deliverance, an end to motion,
and finally built himself a wooden bench to sleep on
surrounded by signs - their shadows on his skin a lullaby
to flesh in a fleshless gallery.

Goldfish

The black fish under the bridge was so long I mistook it
for a goldfish in a Japanese garden the kind the philosophers
wanted about them so much gold underwater to tell them what waited
in another element like breathing water they wanted to go
to the place where closing eyes is to see

I understood the day I closed my eyes in Gifu City I saw Japan
for the first time saw what I had seen the gate to the Nangu
Shrine by the Shinkansen stood straddled before my head and I
held out my hands to touch it and felt changed air it wasn't
there but I walked into it continually and over the gardens full
of pumkin seeds in the ground and wild red flowers over them they
told me

they brought autumn and they were about my head also in Gifu City all
pearled
in mist and happy as Japanese brides. I saw the JR crates on the night
trains that passed through stations and seemed endless and running
on purpose on time's heels on sheer will to cross Honshu one end
to the other money's own messenger fire down the line. And when you
talked me through

Gifu one end to the other eyes closed I saw what I would never
have seen sighted a transvestite taxi driver set apart on the street
a lost person flowers by the pavement pavements for the blind I saw
music as pulled elastic bands drums as the footprints of exacting gods

I mistook the black fish for an oriental goldfish the flash of gold
on its belly meant it carried its message for the element below it
always one storey down Zen masters attaining one storey down and I,
falling into you, story by story, coming to rest in the place where closing
eyes is to see.

Genetics

My father's in my fingers, but my mother's in my palms.
I lift them up and look at them with pleasure -
I know my parents made me by my hands.

They may have been repelled to separate lands,
to separate hemispheres, may sleep with other lovers,
but in me they touch where fingers link to palms.

With nothing left of their togetherness but friends
who quarry for their image by a river,
at least I know their marriage by my hands.

I shape a chapel where a steeple stands.
And when I turn it over,
my father's by my fingers, my mother's by my palms

demure before a priest reciting psalms.
My body is their marriage register.
I re-enact their wedding with my hands.

So take me with you, take up the skin's demands
for mirroring in bodies of the future.
I'll bequeath my fingers, if you bequeath your palms.
We know our parents make us by our hands.

Conor O'Callaghan

Conor O'Callaghan was born in Newry, County Down, in 1968. He grew up in Dundalk, County Louth, where he now lives. He has reviewed extensively, held short-term teaching posts in universities and has written an account of Ireland's world cup soccer debacle, *Red Mist: Roy Keane and the Football Civil War* (Bloomsbury, 2004). His poetry collections are *The History of Rain* (Gallery Press, 1993), *Seatown* (Gallery Press, 1999) and *Fiction* (Gallery Press, 2005).

In *The History of Rain* weather operates as inescapable, literal presence and metaphor for political or social change in Ireland; in *Seatown* the poet's hometown of Dundalk (with its run-down docks, dog-tracks, early houses, housing estates and by-pass) tells a wider history of the end of the twentieth century. This poetry, said to be sceptical or anti-transcendental, has a determined musicality and a persistent ambivalence that amounts to the preservation of fragile possibilities or the mysterious. The existence of self and the fiction of a coherent narrative are tenuous, conditional or qualified: words like "if", "or" and "could" are pivotal in offering options. Even apparently reliable or simple words like "hello" or "fall" have etymological histories which destabilise single, stable meanings. The narrator in this poetry often gives us the slip or barely exists in unanswerable questions, riddles, oblique glimpses (dives into a swimming pool) or answer-phone messages. In 'Sublet' the delicate chain of images define an existence or a coherent narrative as virtually fiction - as objects on the rim or edge of consciousness. The love poems cut their own swathe, avoiding safety, adding variety as spice, to explore love as delicate, luxurious interlude ('River at Night'), erotic ('The Oral Tradition'), humorously sexy ('Green Baize Couplets') or brief interlude ('*'). In 'East' there is the deadpan, anti-romantic, sceptical humour of poetry from Ireland's "unpoetic" coast where the "moon and stars are lost in the lights of the greyhound track"; to read the title poems in *Seatown*, however, is to also experience the possibility of poetry as sanctuary, a place where a constellation of lights on a coalboat can amount to a form of magic that is not reductive to anything other than magic. In *Fiction* language itself generates its own energies, layers, cross-currents, associations and eytomologies which threaten to subvert singular or straightforward readings.

The History of Rain
for Johnny McCabe 1903 - 1993

These are the fields where rain has marched
from time to time. This is the year that
is measured in consistent downpours, until it spills
on the foreground of a basin covered, the tone of dull enamel.

In the half rush to shelter, these unripe blackberries
and woodbine drifts at the level crossing distract a generation
that knows the probability of sitting through August, the blight

of reticence raising a month past an average fall.
Or that later sees the lost patch momentarily bleached
as if by an hour of recorded sun and the history of light.

In the photograph of 1940, my granduncle and his mother.
Late that tall summer they fold their sleeves and step
into the front yard to watch a swarm of veined clouds pass.

As if the full world might still end here,
away from the horizon of more populated storms.

Forgetting that soon they will run back to the house
and the wireless babbling, and listen to the gentle clapping
on slate and galvanised roofs where the sky begins,
suddenly uncertain at the border of an even longer decade.

River at Night
for Vona

We do this at least once a year.
The midges, the cow parsley, the stagnant air

are signposts to the only deep enough pool
after weeks have dried the current to a trickle.

After too much heat, and too much cider,
the night seems forever and the water inviting.

We have walked for miles into unfenced land
where the hum of the distant town is drowned,

and find again that the core of summer
is cold against our sun-burned shoulders.

There's no special way of deciding who goes first.
It just happens that my jeans and tee-shirt

have been left on parched, hoof-marked earth
where a cigarette ripens closer to your mouth.

On the other bank, an orchard and the sky's
expanse spread out like a field of fireflies.

No birdsong, nothing swaying in the high grass,
and little that ties us to what we recognise.

The silence is only disturbed by your voice
saying it can't possibly be so easy,

the planets blossoming. Only the remote throng
of cars at closing time asks if this is wrong.

To forget ourselves and a world more sober.
To forget that the slow persistence of the river

among black horses, black ragwort, black crab-apple trees
is just the brief eternity between two boundaries.

That when we walk this way in a different year
the same sense of longing will still be here.

On the surface of the universe my splashing
and your laughter scarcely make an impression.

After the silence has resumed you say that at some
point we should think of turning back. Come.

For now the night is shining on your arms.
Imagine that we've shaken off the sun and its harness.

Take off your bracelet and your black dress,
and stretch out across the confluence of two days

to where I am floating in darkness.

Seatown

Sanctuary of sorts for the herons all day yesterday
waiting for the estuary to drain and this evening
for two lights queuing like crystal at the top of the bay.

Last straw for the panel beaters only just closed down
and the dole office next to the barracks and the gold
of beer spilled on the pavements of Saturday afternoon.

Home from home for the likes of us and foreign boats
and groups with oilskins and unheard-of currencies
in seach of common ground and teenage prostitutes.

Reclaimed ward of bins left out a week and dogs in heat
and the fragrance of salt and sewage that bleeds
into our garden from the neap-tide of an August night.

Poor man's Latin Quarter of stevedores and an early house
and three huge silos swamped by the small hours
and the buzz of joyriders quite close on the bypass.

Time of life to settle for making a fist of love
and glimpsing new dawns and being caught again
and waking in waves with all the sheets kicked off.

Point of no return for the cattle feed on the wharves
and the old shoreline and the windmill without sails
and time that keeps for no one, least of all ourselves.

May its name be said for as long as it could matter.
Or, failing that, for as long as it takes the pilot
to negotiate the eight kilometres from this to open water.

Landscape with Canal

So this, the means to an end, is chosen
as the landscape of a private fiction
where the tracks you make are all-too-well-known.
Though this time, since whatever will happen
will happen most likely in the open,
you set it in a derelict autumn
when all its symbolic fruit has fallen.
The action is yours alone to govern.
As long as you make the silence broken
by the presence on the bank of someone
that's both anticipated and sudden.
As long as you don't forget to mention
that the voice at once without and your own
is the one that leaves the rest unspoken
and between the past and town has taken
the long way around a simple question.

Say, if you wish, your surrogate father
who charmed the birds in a yard of feathers.
Or say the shade of the young schoolmaster
who sometime during your last free summer
was dumped by his girl for something better
and found with a shotgun two days later
on a disused farm before the border.
The choice is yours - it will scarcely matter.
There'll be in the distance a curfew hour
knelled across the not-so-familiar.
Walking back the shortcut none the wiser
through the mill and the gates of the manor
there must always be some faceless other
on the towpath by the slick of water
who'll call in the murk ahead, 'Who goes there?'
and call once more when you don't quite answer.

Sublet

Within their rented lives I am the gate at all hours,
footsteps on the stairs that might wake their child.
I am a spare set of clothes in the box-room wardrobe,
a misremembered name, the cistern's muffled hum,
a sliver across the landing that widens and shuts over.
I am a temporary measure until things pick up,
a cousin from the west if the landlord asks,
a couple of used notes in advance on the telly
that come as a godsend in the middle of the month.
I am a wafer-thin book that was left by mistake
one weekend on the table, the latest running joke
with her sister, his mother, a reason to whisper.
I am a strange alarm clock, the lukewarm kettle,
a cup no one else uses upside-down by the sink,
the missing inch of milk, a change of plan in red ink
on the back of a napkin. I am a half-minute lull
as the house holds its breath, a rustle in the hall,
the front door slamming onto mid-morning rain.

The Bypass

There are no ships in the
                            docks. It has been raining.
It falls to us like this with each successive week,
the vague sense of being cut adrift or drowning
that sleeplessness accentuates.
                            Then a while back
it dawned on me that we
                            had made our home on land
that is reclaimed. Ever since I have been at sea.
They have cut a bypass over the Lower End,
from the halting sites to
                            the bird sanctuary.

It is the latest in
                    a long stream of removes
from the outside world. It is finished. It crosses
Seatown within earshot of here in even waves
between the tool hire yard
                            and the early houses.
It has given our lives
                    an edge. It's out there now,
going through the motions of distance and darkness,
matter-of-fact, an orchard ripening yellow,
making time and deadlines
                            and mid-summer starless,
a latter-day silk route
                    murmuring with fireflies,
piling itself up at traffic lights, pointillist,
then shifting through its gears, beautiful and tireless,
a droning scarcely
                    audible though always just,
like moths at the window
                            or next door's radio
left running for months, a heavy relentless hum
that quickens past eight and we turn in and wake to,
not once diminishing
                    or losing momentum,
whether hauliers in
                    articulated trucks
or joyriders at speed or motorbikes in swarms
or sirens ebbing on the old shore like tidemarks
or Saturday's tail-back
                            exhaling its sweet fumes,
a necklace lying away
                    out on the marshes
and the mile of disused industrial estates,
linking cities, migrant, a river that washes
its own hands of silence,
                        that dusk accelerates,
that almost dries to a
                    standstill if never quite,
day and night and day and night, not once letting up,

half-dreamt, a buzz constantly in my head of late
and even yet as I

                write. It will never stop.

East

I know it's not playing Gaelic, it's simply not good enough,
to dismiss as someone else's all that elemental Atlantic guff.
And to suggest everything's foreign beyond the proverbial pale
would amount to a classic case of hitting the head on the nail.

But give me a dreary eastern town that isn't vaguely romantic,
where moon and stars are lost in the lights of the greyhound track
and cheering comes to nothing and a flurry of misplaced bets
blanketing the stands at dawn is about as spiritual as its gets.

Where back-to-back estates are peppered with satellite discs
and the sign of the *Sunrise Takeaway* doesn't flick on until six
and billows from the brewery leave a February night for dead
and the thought of smoking seaweed doesn't enter your head.

And while it's taken for granted everyone has relatives in Chicago
who share their grandmother's maiden name and seasonal lumbago,
it's probably worth remembering, at the risk of committing heresy,
as many families in Seatown have people in Blackpool and Jersey.

My own grandmother's uncle ran a Liverpool snooker hall
that cleaned up between the wars and went, of course, to the wall.
I must have a clatter of relatives there or thereabouts still
who have yet to trace their roots and with any luck never will.

I know there's a dubious aunt on my father's side in Blackburn,
a colony on my mother's in Bury called something like Bird or Horn.
I have a cousin a merchant seaman based in darkest St Ives,
another who came on in the seventies for Man. Utd. reserves.

If you're talking about inheritance, let me put it this way:
there's a house with umpteen bedrooms and a view of Dundalk Bay
that if I play it smoothly could be prefaced by the pronoun 'my'
when the old man decides to retire to that big after hours in the sky.

If it comes down to allegiance or a straight choice between
a trickle of shingly beaches that are slightly less than clean
and the rugged western coastline draped in visionary mystique
give me the likes of Bray or Bettystown any day of the week.

If it's just a question of water and some half-baked notion
that the Irish mind is shaped by the passionate swell of the ocean,
I align myself to a dribble of sea that's unspectacular, or flat.
Anything else would be unthinkable. It's as simple as that.

*

I know she knows I still believe
that when she tells him she loves him
there is an asterisk understood after 'love'
and a footnote qualifying her use of the term

for something which never quite measures up
like a storm on record but too long ago
or like an only international cap
in a friendly stopped by snow.

Fall

To unbalance. To keel over, accidentally, or submit to the pressure of gravity
        To plummet in worth, especially currency.
To lose altitude. To take place at some pre-ordained time and date.
        To swallow tall tales at face value.
To lag such a distance back along the trail as to disappear from view.
        To surrender, especially a country
to the enemy camped in its margins for all of two nights and three days.
        To vanish from the radar of grace.
To have no qualms any longer when it comes to telling friends and foes
        alike precisely where to stick
their olive branches. To be the kind of sap who lapses now and then
        into clandestine amorous crushes.
To indulge a whole continent its own broadleaf syllable for autumn.
        To arrive back unexpectedly in the afternoon
and happen upon yourself dancing a single-handed two-step on the landing
        to Bechet's 'As-tu le Cafard?'
To go, especially too far. To leave some unknown pal a shot behind the bar
        and teeter out upon the dawn,
its parabola of stars, as wobbly on your pins as any new-born foal.
        To bolt awake on a balcony
and see the horizon's twinset of Med and azure in a Blinky Palermo abstract
        that has lain open in your lap.
To realise the only part of flight you can handle is the moment after take-off
        into a blank of unmarked blue
when you feel like a kite getting nowhere fast or a balloon strung out on helium.
        To listen to sound effect CDs so often
every track eventually returns to a common denominator called 'wind in trees'.
        To think the hymns of Ulrich Swingli funny.
To praise a glass half-full of homespun pear brandy that tastes of lighter fuel.
        Also to dwell on the bruise
of one dropped apple. Also to descend and keep descending until it becomes
        a sort of *modus vivendi*, a buzz.
Also to stumble and nonetheless to continue, and always to be happy to go down
        in history as anybody's fool,
and somehow to believe in parachutes, and still to find it within you to forgive
        the leaves whatever it is leaves do.

It's for You
from A History of Hello

Blame the blower,
since some kind of formula
for an opening exchange
had to be agreed upon
to get the ball rolling.
And not only for the ears
of polite society,
its upper echelons,
but to trip as readily
from the lips of gigolos
and babes and heathens
and saints and regular Joes.
So, think of the host
of suggested possibilities
grown yellow around the gills
that were dusted down
and duly given the elbow,
that might just as well
have been Hebrew
to the likes of you and me.

Then, think of the 'hillo'
Hamlet shares
with Horatio,
and you're in the general area.
Think of the huntsmaster,
think of the hounds
and a hare's breath,
and you're there or thereabouts.
Think of the troubadour 'hola',
the Huguenot 'salut',
And you're in the same ballpark.
Think of yola as if barked
by the hoodlums of Hanley,
the zealots of Sacramento,

and you're on the right track.
And think also
of Tristram Shandy's 'Hollo! Ho! -
the whole world's asleep! -
bring out the horses - ',
and you're getting warmer.

Pól Ó Muirí

Pól Ó Muirí was born in Belfast in 1965. he was educated at St Mary's Christian Brothers' Grammar School and at Queen's University, Belfast. He has a BA (Hons) in Celtic Studies and Scholastic Philosophy and a PhD in Celtic Studies. He has published six original volumes of poetry in Irish, one collection in English, a collection of short stories in Irish and a biography of Seosamh Mac Grianna in English. He is the author of three novellas for adult learners of Irish and has had four radio plays, in both English and Irish, broadcast on RTÉ. His poetry has been anthologised in: *An Leabhar Mór/The Great Book of Gaelic* (Canongate Books, Edinburgh, 2002); *The Hip Flask: short poems from Ireland* (The Blackstaff Press, Belfast, 2000); *Images & Reflections: photographers and writers seeing our century* (The Linen Hall Library, Belfast, 2000) and *Fearann Pinn* (Coiscéim, Dublin, 2000). He is a journalist by profession.

As befitting a contemporary poet writing in the Irish language, Pól Ó Muirí's work walks the imaginative line of honouring and yet subverting the perceived pieties and conventions of his own half-native, half-adopted tradition. He is a poet of dinnseanchas, yet the lore of place is not of primarily Gaeltacht Ireland but of urbanised - and politicised - West Belfast. Yet Ó Muirí consistently upsets the reader's cultural and political expectations and, in doings so, questions the nature of what it is be 'Irish', 'Nationalist' or, even, a 'Gaeilgeoir'. In his English-language collection D-Day (essentially English-language versions of poems chosen from his first four Irish-language collections) his familial and imaginative muse is generous enough to include those who fought in Second World War serving in the British armed forces. Bangor and Holywood (as well as Dresden and Vietnam) feature as prominently as the Falls Road or the west of Ireland.

A sense of the lone fragile voice endangered by larger forces finds a strange resonance in Ó Muirí's preoccupation with the language itself (or, it could be argued, language itself). While he returns to the subject time and again, his attitudes express a doubting, non-dogmatic sensibility. For example, in 'From the Irish', his stance is almost self-knowingly despairing about the trials of writing in a 'marginal' and arguably 'dying' language: 'I had a vision of myself in 40 years/Walking listlessly down the Loch Road, Lurgan,/A plastic carrier bag held loosely in each despondent hand/And me talking to myself in Irish … '
And yet, in balance to this pessimism, Ó Muirí also writes of the palpable joy in just speaking the words, the mouth music that is the basis of all poetry.

An Damhsóir

Nach go héadrom a iompraíonn do chosa thú,
Tusa atá trí scór go leith, cúraimí an tsaoil
Mar chrois ar bharr croise anuas ar do ghuaillí -
An bhean chithréimeach, an mac ag fáil bháis
Le galar nua-aoiseach nach dtuigeann tú.
Ach le toiseacht an cheoil, béimeann an bhodhráin,
Scréach na fidle, caoineadh cneasta na bpíob,
Tógtar ó na mairbh thú, aiséirí príobháideach
Gach aon oíche, Lazaras an urláir,
Ag rolladh siar carraigeacha d'uaimhe,
Cluineann tú ceol, leathann do mhiongháire:
Aon, dó, trí, ceathair, cúig, sé, seacht,
Aon, dó, trí,
Aon, dó, trí.

Beannchar

Tá trí bliana ó shin, bhí mé sásta
Le turas go Beannchar: mise, mo
Thuismitheoirí, Noel agus Dorothy,
Ag pléidhíocht agus ag lapadaíl ar
Chladaí an Dúin thuaidh.

Seo anois mé go dtí na hascaillí
I ngaineamh mín na Fraince,
Corpáin phollta mo chomrádaithe
Caite thart fúm. Seo an chéad
Uair dom bheith as Éirinn.

The Dancer

How lightly your feet carry you,
You who are three score and ten, life's burdens
Like a cross on top of a cross on your shoulders -
The crippled wife, the son dying of some
New-age disease which you don't understand.
But with the beginning of the music, the beating of the bodhrán,
The screech of the fiddle, the gentle whine of the pipes,
You are raised from the dead, a private resurrection
Every night, Lazarus of the floor,
Rolling back the rocks of your tomb.
And hear the music, your smile widens:
Aon, dó, trí, ceathair, cúig, sé, seacht,
Aon, dó, trí,
Aon, dó, trí.

Bangor

Three years ago, I was happy
With a day trip to Bangor -
Me, my parents, Noel, Dorothy
Messing and splashing
On the beaches of north Down.

Today I am up to my chest
In the holed bodies of my
Friends. This is my first
Time away from Ireland.

Marine

Mí i ndiaidh dó na Dodgers a fhágáil ina dhiaidh
D'iompair an sruth corpán John Connelly, Marine,
Mar rón caillte go cladaí Mhaigh Eo.
Scríobh sagart na paróiste nach ndearnadh lobhadh
Ar an chorp; bhí an t-uisce chomh fuar sin.
"Shíl muid gur ina chodladh ar an trá a bhí sé."
Thóg an tseanmháthair an ghruaim nuair a chan sí:
"Nach iontach go ndearna sé a bhealach féin abhaile?"

Stalingrad

Líne bheag amháin gearrtha
Sa tsioc agus sa tsneachta:
Cordula, kleines Herz, wohin bist du gefahren?
Cordula, a chroí bhig, cá ndeachaigh tú?

Marine

After a month, the tide carried the body of John Connolly, Marine,
Like a lost seal, to the welcoming beaches of Mayo.
The parish priest wrote that the water had been so cold
That the body was perfectly preserved.
We thought, he said, *that he was asleep on the beach.*
The grandmother lifted the gloom when she sang:
Isn't it amazing that he made his own way home?

Stalingrad

One small line cut in the ice and snow:
Cordula, kleines Herz, wohin bist du gefahren?

Cordula, small heart, where have you gone?

Bobby, Wilfred agus Seán

Sa chúigiú bliain chuir muid aithne
Ar Wilfred Owen, Seán O'Casey agus Bobby Sands.
Bhí ár múinteoir Béarla ar theann a dhíchill
Ag cur ar ár súile dúinn gur ag Wilfred agus O'Casey
A bhí an ceart: *A fheara, Dolce et decorum est. Ní fíor.*
Ach bhí Bobby Sands i ndiaidh bás a fháil
Agus ní raibh muid cinnte.
San amharclann, dúirt an t-óglach:
Boyle, no man can do enough for Ireland.
Lig muid asainn búir a thóg na fraitheacha
A chuir in iúl do na scoltacha Protastúnacha
Gur ann dúinn, go raibh muid éirithe
Dár nglúine agus go mbeadh go deo.
Wilfred bocht.
Cad é mar a thiocfadh linn
Cluas le héisteacht a thabhairt dó
Agus cónra ar chónra ag triall
Síos trinsí ár sráideanna?
O'Casey bocht.
Dar linn gur ag an óglach a bhí an ceart.
Johnny Boyle, ní raibh ann ach
Scrublach de fhealltóir.
Ba muid na fir chrua na laetha úd.

Bobby, Wilfred and Seán

In fifth-year we met
Wilfred Owen, Seán O'Casey and Bobby Sands.
Our English teacher did his best
To show us that Wilfred and Seán were right:
Ah, lads, Dulce et decorum est. *It isn't true.*
But Bobby Sands was after dying
And we weren't too sure.
In the theatre, the volunteer said:
Boyle, no man can do enough for Ireland.
We let out a roar which lifted the rafters
Just to let the Protestant schools know
That we were there, that we had risen from our knees
Now and forever.
Poor Wilfred.
How could we listen to him
While coffin after coffin trialled
Down the trenches of our streets?
Poor O'Casey.
We thought that the volunteer had it right -
Johnny Boyle was nothing but
A waster of a traitor.
We were the hard men those days.

Turas tacsaí

Agus muid leath bealaigh suas Bóthar na bhFál
Cuireann an tiománaí óg tacsaí ceist orm:
An tú fear an pháipéir?
Baineann a chuid Gaeilge geit asam
Agus canann muid linn i nGaeilge gharbh na bhFál
Fá Thír Chonaill, fán iomáint, fán pholaitíocht
Go gcailltear i gceo ár gcainte trácht is beairic.

Calafort

Áit inteacht idir Loch Feabhail agus Murmansk
cuireadh do bhád go grinneall na farraige
tásc ná tuairisc ar do chorp ní bhfuarthas
bratach náisiúnta ar chónra níor dreapaíodh
siúlóid an Twelfth nó Féile Pádraig ní dhearnadh arís
áit inteacht idir Loch Feabhail agus Murmansk
ar shaoistí líonta na farraige
tá do thaibhse bhriste ar snámh.

The Paper Fella

Half-way up the Falls -
That is neither upper nor lower whack -
The young taxi driver questions me:
Are you the paper fella?
His Irish startles me
And we sing in rough Falls Irish
About Donegal, hurling, politics,
Until traffic and barrack are lost
In the mist of our speech.

Harbour

Somewhere between Loch Foyle and Murmansk,
Your ship was sent to the seabed.
No trace of your body was found,
No national flag on a coffin was draped.
The 12th or St Patrick's was walked no more.
Somewhere between Loch Foyle and Murmansk,
On the full rollers of the ocean,
Your broken ghost is afloat.

Faire na Reilige

Ós tú an corp deireanach sa reilig
Tugtar ort í a fhaire
Go dtí go dtig an chéad mharbhán eile.
Ualach trom an coimhéad ag girseach óg -
Ag míniú do bhunadh na n-uaigheanna
Gach aon scéal úr agus iontach.
Ba cheart go mbeifeá san fhaisean is déanaí
Ag damhsa ar urlár dioscó, ag suirí le spraoi,
Ag seachaint na ngasúr, ag cúlchaint le cairde,
Agus ní ag siúl ó leacht go tuama
Ar fud na cille.

Casey Jones

Léim m'athair mór le fuinneamh an balla cúil
agus é ag éalú ar an RUC thiar i 1942:
Bhí siad ag piocadh na bpiléar as ár ngairdín
go ceann bliantaí ina dhiaidh sin, a chuimhnigh m'uncail -
síoltaí beaga a d'fhásfadh agus a bhláthfadh i dtrátha an ama
a phreab m'athair mór, bricliath uasal,
mise ar a ghlúin agus é ag coimhéad liom Casey Jones,
dúil ainmheasartha an iarthiománaí traenach
á léiriú féin i ngach siolla den chnúdán
a rinne muid as béal a chéile:
Casey Jones, a-steaming and a-rolling.

Watcher

As you are the last body in the graveyard,
It is your duty to watch over it
Until the next corpse comes.
This watching is a heavy burden
For a young girl -
Telling people of the graves
Everything strange and startling.
You should be in the latest fashion
Dancing on a disco floor,
Avoiding the boys, gossiping,
And not walking from gravestone to tomb
Throughout the churchyard.

Casey Jones

My grandfather jumped this wall with verve,
Escaping from the RUC back in 1942:
They were picking bullets from our garden
For years after that, my uncle recalled -
Small seeds which would sprout and flower
About the time
My grandfather, grey and noble, bounced
Me on his knee as he watched with me
Casey Jones,
The uncontrolled passion of the ex-train driver
Revealing itself in every syllable
As we purred together:
Casey Jones, a-steamin' and a-rollin' ...

Taise/Fís

i

Mar thaise, bhog tú fríd an oíche ó theach go teach go hantráthach.
Shiúil tú isteach thar thairseach gan iarraidh - níor smaointigh tú
Ar chnag a bhuaileadh; níor nós den phobal é (nó sin a shíl tú).
Scanraigh tú mná na dtithe cé nach raibh de dhíobháil ort
Ach gloine bainne, nó tae, má bhí an ciotal thíos.

Dúradh fosta gur ghnách leat labhairt leat féin:
Chonacthas thíos ar an chladach ag monamar thú,
Comhartha mire, gan aon amhras.
Faoi dheireadh, tógadh faoi rún as an cheantar thú
Agus, nuair a thiteann an cholch dheireanach den bhallóg,
Ligfidh an pobal osna fhaoisimh.
Ach bogfaidh tú go fóill mar thaise inár measc.

ii

Chonaic mé mé féin i gceann dhá scór bliain
Ag siúl go líodránta síos Bóthar na Locha, an Lorgain,
Mála plaisteach earraí go scaoilte i ngach aon lámh
Éadóchasach agus mé ag siosarnach liom féin
I nGaeilge, ag féacháil le haibhleogaí na teanga sin -
Briathra, aidiachtaí, nathanna - a athfhadú.
As stóras mo chuimhne chaith mé fód
Abairtí agus ghuigh go mbéarfadh
Na haibhleogaí ar an lón anama,
Go bpléascfadh an tine chun beatha
Mar a phléasc tráth.

From the Irish

I

Like a ghost, you moved through the night
From house to house at a late hour.
You walked in across the threshold without bidding -
You would not have thought to knock:
It was not your people's custom.
You frightened the women of the house
Whose men were away in Scotland
But all you wanted was a glass of milk or tea
If the kettle were down.
It was said that you used to speak to yourself,
You were seen on the shore mummering,
A sign of madness, no doubt.
You were banished from the area
And when the last stone falls
From the ruin of your family home
The people will let loose a sigh.

II

I had a vision of myself in 40 years
Walking listlessly down the Loch Road, Lurgan,
A plastic carrier bag held loosely in each despondent hand
And me talking to myself in Irish,
Trying to rekindle the cinders of that language -
Verbs, adjectives, sayings -
Throwing another sod of sentences from my memory's store
And praying that the cinders will catch this load;
That the fire will crackle into life
As it did once.

Adrian Rice

Adrian Rice was born in Belfast, County Antrim, in 1958. His first published sequence of poems was a collaboration with the artist Ross Wilson in a limited edition box set, *Muck Island* (1990). In addition to editing the anthology *Signals* (Abbey Press, 1997), he has compiled collections of children's poetry, art, and drama - *Life of the Lough* (1999), *Sea and Shore* (2000), *Around the Lough* (2001), *Loughviews* (2003) and *Shorelines* (2004) - and anthologies entitled *A Conversation Piece: Poetry and Art* (Ulster Museum & Abbey Press, 2002) and *The Tin God: A History of the Cans Metal Box factory* (Cans Metal Box Pensioner's Club, Portadown, 2002). His two collections of poetry are *Impediments* (Abbey Press, 1997) and *The Mason's Tongue* (Abbey Press, 1999). A new volume, *The Moongate Sonnets*, is forthcoming. He is currently Adjunct Professor of English at Lenoir-Rhyne College in North Carolina.

Adrian Rice's poetry dissects Northern Protestantism with rigour, clarity and balance; the constrictions and liberations of this tradition are revealed, celebrated and satirised. If "The Protestant heart is a zoo of lust" or rock solid in unwavering political machismo - "Hand on the tribal batons/And to Hell with hope?/Trumpet-tongued, the grim graffito -/FUCK THE NEXT POPE." - then it is also, in 'The Changeful Tap', able to celebrate through understatement, individualism and the lore of place as alternative sources of strength. The examination of the poet's community, from the historic Antrim coast of Islandmagee to the contemporary urban fringes of Belfast in Rathcoole, is undertaken with telling accuracy and the use of minute detail; there is an ear for native North Antrim idiom and an eye for mystery (revealed in 'Green Light') in the poetry. A summary of the poet's gloss on words in the poems may assist the reader: Rosebrook was the poet's maternal grandparents' timber-framed bungalow in Newtownabbey; the KAI are Rathcoole Loyalists and their marching band, an acronym for 'Kill All Irish'; Jah-Bul-On is a composite word in the Masonic Order for Jahweh, Baal, and Osiris; The Wing was Thomas Hill, 1759-1821, a schoolmaster from Islandmagee (of slight build and mercurial disposition) and William McClelland was an Islandmagee man wrongly blamed in 1814 for circulating a story about a captured mermaid at Portmuck.

The Big Picture

for Raymond Armstrong

Outside the window,
B-movie rain falls in floods.
Someone must be on my roof,
Sending those buckets down.

Other hands have the house surrounded
With cranes and booms;
The gardens tracked,
The cameras dollying along.

While the key grip corners the gaffer,
The continuity girl works
With an awkward shoe,
And the best boy does what best boys do.

I suppose they are waiting on me.
Well, they can wait.
I'm not coming out.
What's happening is happening inside.

Rosebrook

in memory of Louisa Hay

Sky-floor is rumbling:
'God shifting His furniture'.
The heavens open.

*

Rosebrook awash. As
The wind lifts, the house creaks like
An old galleon.

*

A real ripsnorter:
A wind-scythe through tidy beds -
Funeral flowers.

*

Miraculously,
Each Kerry blue slate up and
Landed like a leaf.

*

Poles standing, knock-kneed;
Lines sagging like necklaces:
Bird-bead abaci.

*

Watching the birdies,
A soggy cat plucks netted-
Wire like a harpist.

*

A double-yolk sun
Setting over steaming fields.
Promising weather.

The Dummy Fluter

Huffin' and puffin', pursin' and poutin',
Struttin' his stuff at the back of the band:
'Lips', 'Dog Whistle', 'Fingers' and *'Golden'* -
The 'team' wouldn't travel without him.

No Orange credential or way with the flute
Secures him a place in this loyalist troupe.
He could be a KAIser; a slick womaniser;
The club raconteur or the site racketeer;

Somebody's son or Somebody's brother;
Or a bit of a bastard who hammers the beer.
But when all's said and done, more often than not,
This master of no tune is basically HARD:

Hard on his Ma, hard on his Da,
Hard on his brothers and sisters and girl;
Hard on his teachers, hard on the preachers,
And hard on your face should you cross him at all.

Silent Argument

for Ian Duhig

It is not unheard of for me to entrust
My barnet to the hands of a barber
Who has years since lost his hearing.

And I have noticed how he seems more
Than a trifle nervous when his friends
Appear for a short-back-and-sides.

In ear-splitting whispers, he reveals that unless
He delivers a cut-above-the rest, they never cease
Talking about him at the club for the deaf.

Hold Back the Cauldrons

And as we look out
From the ramparts,
We all ask,
'Whose poem is the greatest?'

Now he's not saying this because
So-and-so's here - however;
He says,
So-and-so is the greatest,
Packed with originality and power.

Well, since he's not saying
That yours or yours
Is less than great,
Then we all nod
And yes yes
As we gladly agree
That So-and-so's is surely

One of the greatest poems
Anyone has seen
In a long, long time.

Then while
The (wonderful! wonderful!)
Poem is read,
Some bear gentle
Smiles
And someone even
Cries.

So there it is.
Keep the gates shut.
Be vigilant.
But hold back the cauldrons
Of boiling oil.

The Mason's Tongue

Although a likeable, charitable soul,
He had a less than secret tongue;
So it was removed, and entombed
A ritual distance from the shore -
Sealed dumb in the packed sand.

When a young man dug it up
(Out toiling for some bait)
It dropped from the wet spade
On to the cool slab of strand,
And lay like an odd curl of meat.

The young man cupped it in his hands
To get a closer look,
When, stirring on his palms
And with a strangely mournful note,

It suddenly began to speak:

Go tell all the brethren
There is no rest where I have gone,
No answer comes from Jah-Bul-On.

Bewildered, and seized with sudden dread,
He let the tongue flop to the sand,
Then scooped it back up with his spade
And flung it out across the waves.
Yet, though hushed upon the ocean bed,
The tongue's words lapped about his head:

Go tell all the brethren
There is no rest where I have gone,
No answer comes from Jah-Bul-On.

Green Light

Crouching like a fada
On top of the hill
A dark figure
Watches for a signal.

Fireguards

Changed overnight from sulky schoolkids
To tinder-hunters and rag-and-bone boys,
We slogged for weeks to build the blaze.

We bore trees like trophies from Carnmoney Hill
And hauled household junk from airless attics.
We dragged behind us the bed-wetter's mattress,

Leaving a trail like a huge slug's slither,
And palm-rolled dozens of baldy tyres
From fusty coalsheds and skittered yards.

As the bonfire rose like a wooden wigwam,
We caught the vision of a dodgy den:
We put a door in the bonfire's side

And carpeted a generous circle of grass
With scullery lino and cardboard strips
To beat the damp and the feared earwig.

Kitchen-drawer candles or hurricane lamps -
Swiped in the night from roadwork sites -
Brought to light the tell-tale litter

Of Coke cans, crisp-bags, cheap beer tins,
Nude-book pages and wet fag-ends,
Ruined Rizlas and lemonades from Yacht:

Refundable bottles religiously retrieved,
While the rest was abandoned to burn.
Although sometimes used as a lewd laboratory -

You show me yours and I'll show you mine -
The den was mostly a male preserve.
Whether the sun was splitting the sky

Or fog rolled in like liquid floss
Or a redbrick moon capped chimney-tops,
We sat in and looked out on painted kerbs,

Flag-draped houses and maisonettes.
Well-armed with hatchets, knives and sticks,
We guarded the bonfire from arson attacks.

The Wing

for Samuel Thompson

A blush of sunset lights the path
To the Wing's at Ballywindy, Mullaghdubh,
For a legendary scene in the island's history:
The undertaker's nightmare - a bodiless wake.

The Wing had disappeared without trace.
One moment the hubble-bubble of *Macbeth;*
The next, gone -
Pupils left admiring and agog.
Within his alphabet of eccentricity,
This was surely the Z.

While warm fadge and tea were passed round,
Some thought McAlshinder was spot on:
He was a clubbable little man, all over you
Like a badly cut suit. Those seashell ears,
And that composite face - plain, ample markers
For anyone. It's simple - he's ghosted back under the hill.

Yet anxious in a corner sat old McClelland,
Puzzling what the Wing had said:
Though I love this tongue-of-land, I've made up my mind...
And he spoke of her swimming in
From the heart of the sea, top-half fully bared,
Cradling her catch of oysters and pearls.

McClelland, you knew him better than anyone did.
What's your verdict?
Well, what could he say?
Fairies under Muldersleigh Hill seemed outlandish enough;
How then could he tell them -
'He's away with the Mermaid'?

Out and up the dark hill towards home,
With only a backward glance
At the scarf of smoke from the chimney-top,
Raising a laugh at the memory of the Wing,
Sweep's brush floundering about in the summer air -
Entirely useless:
McClelland, if the moon had been out
We'd have darkened its face.
- Yes, Wing... we'd have darkened its face.

The Changeful Tap
from Sorrow-Songs

The water would suddenly thin to a trickle,
Some summer evenings while filling the kettle -
It took an eternity just to make tea.
And I'd know with an absolute certainty
He'd made his way back to the garden
To toddle around the immaculate rows,
To sprinkle the heads of infant flowers
From the font of his watering can.
It was such chores that kept him happy.
Still, I'd secretly curse our shared supply
And covet the moment when I'd have control.
But nowadays reaching to turn on the tap,
I sometimes fall for the futile hope
The running water might suddenly slow.

Frank Sewell

Frank Sewell was born in Nottingham in 1968 and grew up in Belfast. He studied English and Russian at Queen's University and received a Ph.D. in Irish Poetry from the University of Ulster at Coleraine where he now teaches. Frank Sewell has written literary criticism such as *Modern Irish Poetry: A New Alhambra* (OUP, 2000), translated Irish language poems in Cathal Ó Searcaigh's *By the Hearth in Mín a' Leá* (Arc Publications, 2005) and co-edited *Artwords: an Ulster anthology of contemporary visual art and poetry* (Cranagh Press. 1999). His poetry publications include *Outside the Walls: Poems by Frank Sewell & Francis O'Hare* (An Clochán,1997) and *How the Light Gets In* (Cranagh Press, 1999); Sewell has also translated, with Mitsuko Ohno, *On Two Shores*, poems from the Japanese of Mutsuo Takahashi (Dedalus, 2006).

Frank Sewell's poetry uses uncertainty to energise creativity, to accommodate song and loss. The poetry acknowledges and converses with both musical predecessors (the song 'River deep, mountain high' or Van Morrison in 'Madame Elena') and literary forerunners (through linguistic echo or context) but it also adds new takes and tunes and polishes "rusty daggers". The bleak north coast, for instance, is the backdrop to a dialogue with Seán Ó Ríordáin and those who have "flickered since Joyce/took language, lit the face of her/and showed us up in words". Poems often make a virtue of the certainty of uncertainty. 'Not knowing where you stand' and 'Hands' reflect on the tenuous virtues, perhaps necessities, of not standing on solid ground or rushing to judgements, of the left hand not knowing what the right is doing. 'A Rusty Dagger' knows that neither staying nor going from the North of the Troubles would have produced either the certainty of belonging or a stable, detached vision - just a relative one. The chosen light that signals in these poems is intermittent; the pronouns used alternate and shift. Love's specific transience and fragility but universal recurrence inform poems about relationships; as time alters, messages on headboards, inside wallets - even on the walls of West Belfast - alter too. This poetry, then, is a sensitive register of how necessary adjustments in time and irreconcilable loss coexist; this poetry knows today's important messages are often truncated tomorrow, or found, before long, in the folds of the sofa before they are lost for good.

Not knowing where you stand

Not knowing where you stand
is where you stand;
always wanting to put your foot down
on dry land and not finding it
or, when you do, not standing it,
sailing on until you change
your mind, turn back and find it gone.

Is it under a pebble or stone
scooped up and dropped into the ocean,
your one-and-only chance
which when recognised as such
hightails it? Where do you stand
when you're too far gone to judge
the swell of the sea, the lie of the land?

Walking the dog

From RPG Avenue to the Falls Road in the '80s,
I turn where trees and street-lights
stand like giant sentries.

My dog (a revisionist)
pisses on their shoes,
sniffs the recent past

of the pavement, then gives it dog's abuse.
Inscriptions, chalked, scratched, painted,
make the road a text. Here, 'the fools,

the fools...' has been ended
by a paint-bomb; both will be replaced,
the offence re-offended.

The wall around Our Lady's Hospice,
like a book
read under blankets,

torched in the neon look
of cars' glancing headlights,
lunges from the black

(white letters) DON'T LET THEM DIE.
I have to think hard
before the Hunger Strike

fleshes the words
with context.
My dog's perked ears guard

the metre of my steps.
Deep in his night-dark coat,
he breathes hot hoary wisps

of impatience with the road's,
and my own, meandering.
Hungry for the park, he strolls

on as if nothing
should keep a dog from grass.
And I follow him, walking

slowly, just in case
there is something
I can learn from all this

other than the scoring
of old scores - SAS
three, IRA nothing

and vice versas
over and over again
until the Falls Road falls

flat on its name
and the park seems a small
consolation buried under rain,

the writing on the wall.

For Seán Ó Ríordáin

I

Remember the days
you could hang a poem
on the sun's rays?
You didn't give a damn,
it was that natural.
Verse flew through you
like a dose of salts
or a bad flu,
making you cough
shadows from your lungs.
More reason than enough
to spit, you sung.

II

Dark, there from day one,
lets there be light.
Inherence - is that it?
The way there's no ocean
except where stones cut
waves like a vandal's knife
or the bulb over this hut
flicks on/off all night?
Here's a black spot, Sean.
Are you following me?

I could have sworn…
What about the pub for company?
No, you're right about that.
Not worth a shilling,
the half-words and -thoughts
passed in lieu of conversation
there. Who am I telling?
I like this outdoor condensation,
the wind slugging my coat
and hat, the night pitch-black
and you following me about.
Cohen says everything's cracked,
that's how the light gets in.
Look, that bulb flashing
bright-not-bright again,
the tipsy rain dancing
on The Anchor, the boats,
the naff bedighted lamp-posts
and shops watching from the prom
the on/off/on/off/on
of a beaming, being, breathing
absence, presence of light
that keeps coming or leaving -
it's too hard to decide
with no tense in English
for the bíonn/ní bhíonn
there still be's in Irish
from Gaoth Dobhair to Dún Chaoin.

III

Sean, Galltacht and Gaeltacht
speak a forked tongue.
It's for priests, not poets,
to chant a plain song.

Listen, can I be honest?
I learnt from Ó Direáin
to learn from Yeats,
and still I am learning

from fathers and artificers
who have flickered since Joyce
took language, lit the face of her
and showed us up in words.

Madame Elena, 30th Avenue

They say it's a sin but I paid
Madame Elena 15 bucks to let me in
to her secret chamber; the walls red,
candles on the table at either end.

What I remember from here dims
to one scene: a life-size Christ
not up where you'd expect to find him
but laid flat out to be washed and dressed.

Did I fancy myself as that Christ-figure,
naked, his wounds open to the world?
Yes, or rather, I felt transfigured
by his celebrated heart, his crown of thorns.

'I read palms, cards or tea leaves.
It's up to you.' How could I decide?
'Whatever's the best. You tell me.'
'The cards. The cards,' she replied.

There I was, lost in the mists,
needing Madame Elena to see me through.
Of all she said I remember only this:
'there's darkness all around but light in you'.

I loved her for seeing good in me.
Even if she was a tarted-up charlatan
whose prophecy boiled down to what will be
will be, what is done is done,

I rose, washed and dressed, and kept on.

'River deep, mountain high'

They say I shouldn't love you anymore.
Forget and move on. Move on and forget.
Not to do so is retarded development.
(Everyone's a psychologist these days.)
But what do they know about it?
How many of them had you to love?

Now they say shake yourself out of it
like a dog the river off its back.
But it isn't as easy as that to stop
on the gripless slopes of a mountain
too high and valley too low to keep
me from you. The river runs deep.

Hands

One hand so loved sand,
he cupped himself around
as many of the golden grains
as he thought he could contain.

On guard against loss,
his fingers grew solid as walls,
his palms hard as prison floors,
his thumb shut tight as the door.

Even then, sand breezed
through the cracks, released
itself to the open air, drifted
to the beach. The hand stiffened.

Feeling his hoard, once soft,
unfill his grasp and grow rough,
he tightened his hold and clasped
together joints, folds, gaps,

so hard he sensed every loss.
His efforts crushed and forced
the last of his treasure
away. Easing the pressure,

his wrist sagged with relief,
fingers, half-dead or asleep,
stretched out, his thumb woke.
Fingernails to palm, he shook.

Sand fell away from him
inevitably as time,
and he was left as if
losing was his life.

Another hand so loved sand
he held it loosely for a moment,
then let it go, free.
The hand was soon empty

and himself free to hold
more sand; not the old
grains scattered to the winds
but infinitely varied combinations

again and again until
he embraced the cold thrill
of empty space, the freedom
and the contrast it gave him.

A rusty dagger

('Odi atque amo:
Shall we cut this name on trees with a rusty dagger?'
Louis MacNeice, *Autumn Journal*)

I have stayed behind,
been ready for the off
and changed my mind.
This'll make you laugh.
I planned my exile
in Stirling first of all,
to leave one Celtic mile
for another. The soil
of the Saxon foe
was no go. No go
at all in the end,
I stayed behind
and half-lived it
bomb by bomb
and still what is meant
by home, I can't fathom.
The people on the road,
am I theirs?
Are they my own?
Who-to-hell cares?
They don't, so why…?
Home. Home.
We kick it around
like a stone and go
back at Christmas
but it never works,
the knives and forks
are set against us:
the family reunion,
the national anthem,
the queen's speech,
the papal visit,
just go to show
what a misfit
you are,
what a wretch,
and how much
you aren't
home

Your pelt pyjamas

are small
but beautiful
the breast pockets
full of change
and the trousers
always manage
to wind up
tucked into
my own
the two
woven
into one
at the waist
feet or knee
not that this
is any kind
of complaint
believe me
whatever it is
going on
between your
pelt pyjamas
and my own
I don't want
undone

Falling out

of a cereal packet
onto our kitchen table
- the alphabet.

You or I,
I don't know which,
placed a few letters
of the sticky-backed script

onto the headboard
of our single bed:
I LOVE YOU,
just over our heads.

Through wear and tear,
and tear and wear,
U fell away
and the legend everafter

was cut short to
I LOVE YO.
Who's the Chinaman?,
I used to joke,

making out U
had slipped off
with another.
You used to laugh

and so did I.
Now neither you nor I
rest so assured
or live out any

such legend.
Perhaps the legendary

outlives us.
If you and / or I

were to one day
drop
into our old apartment,
climb back up

the long flight of stairs
perhaps there
on the headboard,
the letters

L,O,V, and E
would have clung on;
perhaps there in the bed,
some Chinaman and woman.

To my love with all my love forever

written bold on a pink square of paper
and laminated (can you believe it? *laminated*)
to last, cocooned in a see-through wrapper,

clingfilmed like a left-over sandwich
or the ten square millimetres of cheese
you called me Ben Gunn for keeping in the fridge.

I can't help it, wanting to preserve,
eke things out, rehash the remnants
and make a meal of it, an *hors d-oeuvre*

or just dessert for handing you over
my love with all my love forever.
For what? Some photo or scrap of paper

I kept religiously in my wallet
until it went absent like your own
memento amoris or whatever you called it?

*

And now that's it.
We don't need reminders of each other
from one year to the next.

It's only when looking for
lost keys, i.d., or money
down the sofa

that I / you / we suddenly
find and put them away again.
One day

you look, and they're gone.
The last sign.
The final token.

Cherry Smyth

Cherry Smyth was born in 1960. She grew up in Portstewart, County Derry, became a student at Trinity College Dublin, and undertook post-graduate research in Film and Television Studies at Middlesex University, London. She currently lives in London and teaches creative writing to adults and prisoners. Smyth is the author of two non-fiction books, *Damn Fine Art by New Lesbian Artists* (Cassell, 1996), and *Queer Notions* (Scarlet Press, 1992). Her fiction was included in the *Anchor Book of New Irish Writing* (Anchor 2000); her collection of poetry is entitled *When The Lights Go Up* (Lagan Press, 2001).

Cherry Smyth's poetry combines the courageously sensual and combative to question conservative ideas of sexuality, politics and gender politics. Smyth has spoken of writing as a difficult attempt to (re)claim personal and "Irish and Protestant" identities from the perspective of a northern, lesbian, atheist poet (*In the Chair*, Salmon Press, 2002). Smyth's poetry explores complex, simultaneous realities; the poems which reflect on growing up with the Troubles concisely, sometimes grimly, mirror the way that chilling brutality and the lovingly "normal" co-exist. The love poems frequently explore the acute difficulties and intimate pleasures of lesbian relationships. Smyth's 'Area of Detail' paper, delivered at Cork University (2001), refers to writing as "creating family. On my own terms." Acknowledged influences on the work are "incorrigibly plural"; Irish poets (Seamus Heaney, Louis MacNeice, Eavan Boland); African-American prose writers (Toni Morrison); screenwriters (Marguerite Duras); theorists (from Sartre to Julia Kristeva) and film directors (John Cassavetes). The poetry not only deftly manages to encompass the spectrum of language levels, it also maintains an especially fine balance between wry, vernacular speech, telling detail and lyrical economy. A combination of embrace and renunciation also makes this poetry dynamic, transgressive and bracing. As U.A. Fanthorpe writes: "This is a fierce, economical poetry, picking its way through difficult country....Small things, like a black leather jacket, and 'pretty manicured nails', tell, brokenly, stories of deep significance, and often deep hurt. This is exciting work..."

Maybe it was 1970

Kids my age play real soldiers,
dashing milk bottle bombs against tanks,
binlids for shields.
'That gun's as big as thon wee skitter.'
Mummy turns up the sound.
I'm missing 'Crossroads',
leave the room loudly
and slip behind the kitchen curtain
to search for Derry burning.
The news is too far away.

Maybe it was 1970.
Bernadette Devlin shouting.
She was a student and she was a MP.
She was a cheeky wee monkey.

On the news Dad's shop burning
down. My mascara had run.

Maybe it was 1973.
The Reverend Ian Paisley
crushed through a window on the telly.
His hand bled.
'For God's sake, this is madness. Go home.'
How could a minister be bad?
Blood ran freely down his wrist
like roads, like the Red Hand of Ulster,
severed.

I was fifteen.
Miss Duffin announced in assembly,
'If this doesn't stop very soon,
it's double maths on Friday afternoon.'
The bombscares stopped.

Maybe it was 1977.
On the news Dad's shop burning down.
I was at Kelly's.
It came on in the bar.
I was in love with Shawn Logan.

I didn't know whether to kiss or cry.
I wanted him. I wanted to go home.
He was much older. He was a Catholic.
He held me in his car. It was a BMW.

He tried to touch me. 'Don't,' I said.
'I've got a Tampax in.' But I wanted him.
His words were pure love,
'I don't mind,' he said. My mascara had run.
I should have gone home.

Not everything was destroyed.
That was worse. They sold the damage,
salvaging charred dresses, odd shoes,
scalded mannequins. Everything rained on.
Shawn chewed chewing gum. So did I.

I looked at faces differently.
Daddy was quiet for a long time.

Strange Bed

Sleeping in a strange bed,
its singleness takes me home,
freshly ironed sheets and ribbon-edged blankets,
accept my body with its dried, musk sweat.
If you were here I would rest my head
on your right shoulder, curl my knee

under your thighs. We would sleep unaware
of narrowness, turn and touch
through unremembered dreams
and wake murmuring, I love you.
You would enjoy the faded quilt
of pale green seahorses and regular roses,

its cotton plumpness, uneven,
comforting, and laugh with me
about the tyranny of duvets.
If you could hold me I could sleep,
I could settle now, go over, go down.
If you were here I would sleep.

Family Tree

In the morning my lover has tea with her mother.
I am in her little girl's bed, the daughter's bed, baby sister's bed.
This gives me a delicious frisson to be so near her past,
her childhood, when she still believed she was a boy.
I pretend to be asleep, wish I was invisible
or had a huge cock between my legs.
Why is it so hard to be welcomed,
to be just what they wanted for their little Beth Ann?
I have come to know that no matter how charming,
polite, friendly, feminine or masculine I am,
I will never be good enough, for I am not a man.

Framed on the wall is a family tree,
which stretches back four generations:
the Daidones, the Johnsons, the Prestias, the Spinellis,
the Caferellis, the Morrisons, the McDonalds, the Damms.
Everyone is married off, has been given branches,
but my lover. The tree stops with her.

I want to give her a baby now. I want to have hers now.
I will be on that tree. I hate that tree
and want to sabotage it for I know its branches
will never extend to us. I hate that tree.

A Real Phone

I want a real phone.
A big square one
that rings through the house,
not a trim oblong
of a phone that shrills.

I want a round dial
that spins slowly
through the numbers
making long distance
seem very far away,
not easy fingertip
buttons that beep
connections instantly.

I want a real phone,
one with a receiver
that I can hang up if I need to,
not a phone that you set down when finished.
There's no finality to that.
No abrupt tring.
No satisfying statement.

I want a real phone.

Cotton Vest

I love your white,
100% cotton, ribbed vest.
It sits just right on your shoulders,
straps define the bone,
the bump of muscle.
It scoops your chest,
entices hands to cup breasts.
The nipples say hello.

You laugh when I iron it,
point the hot nose down
its neat edges, make the creases
all march the same way.
'No one sees it,' you say.
But I want its freshness
to be good next your skin,
close over your taut belly,

warm on your long back,
when my body is not there.
Cool nights you keep it on,
smelling of day sweat and fresh garlic.
I curl my fingers under its cover and sleep
or need to feel skin so much
I unpack you, draw the vest up and over,
toss it crumpled to the floor.

When The Lights Go Up

You promise a beginning, like the smooth
opening of long, dark drapes
in the cinema, which whisper,
'I will take all your pain away.'

When I hear your red Rover
change into third at the bottom of our hill
it seems to growl like the MGM lion,
'I will make you insatiable.'

You laugh when I haven't been funny, your laugh,
smoky as Talisker and feed me salted popcorn,
glazed with butter and gunpowder.
Your eyes burn and flicker, 'I will show you a good time.'

You bathe me in rosemary,
wrap me in a thin blanket of new skin
and call softly from a black and white film,
'You are the most beautiful thing I have ever seen.'

I could almost feel the ground slip,
your palm settle on my brow, taste your melted chocolate,
almost eat your baked vanilla buns,
believe you when you say, 'Believe me.'

But when the phone rings after midnight,
I let it ring.

Lost

Me and my own devices head
between the thorn hedges of Antrim
in the dead of night.
The trees are black and bare, lashed with rain.
The shortcut fails again. I will not turn around.
This road will come back to me.
I wonder what Ballycastle looks like,
empty and quiet but for the sea.
There are no truckstops, no overhead signs.
I can't read the bend in the road.

Too many freeways have guided me.
The petrol light blinks like a red star.
Past the scan of the headlights lies true darkness,
an atmosphere of fields and sheep
and people turning in their sleep.
This is what I wanted, to be beyond love's radar,
in the obedient company of a car,
with no navigator. I drive into vacancy
rendering distance and a good loneliness,
a full reliquary in the boot.

In The South That Winter

We both went a little crazy in the South that winter
and now we can admit it, now that it's over
and we've come through and I'm crossing the Hudson on a train.
I remember running from our bed to lie on the wee bed
in the study, in a sleeping bag, which smelt of sand
and dust and someone else's sleep,
and beating it on my thighs till feathers
broke loose and my cries were white.
You tried to stop me, frightened by the sounds I made,
your hands placed where anger would not place them.
You must have wanted to show blood
for you smashed the beloved, shipped china cabinet,
and tore up the Couple's book I bought to save us.
Pages lay in an intimacy of blood and glass.

We both claimed the most injury.
Boy, does every love contain such hate?
Yet here I am, not fresh as a daisy, more like
a full, fat rose whose petals curl brown at the edges,
but whose stem is thick, a thorned artery deep in the earth,
or a sunflower, clustered with seeds, its dishevelled head
a little heavy after a blistering summer in full field.

For you, the day after, fist bandaged, had dragged
garden furniture on to the beach before I got up,
made breakfast and led me to the water,
to sit and eat in the light with you, like queens,
perfectly calm and perfectly happy.
People walking past could see how in love we were
and wanted a place at our white table.

Keeping Ireland Clean

The woman in the Doohat Post Office
wears three differently-necked acrylic sweaters,
a red cotton skirt, no tights,
or socks and soiled black brogues.

She tells me that when a cow breaks a leg,
you ring for the dead lorry.
A man comes with a shotgun and chains
and you pay him to take the heifer away.

At one time, she says, he paid you.
You can't just bury the cattle in the ground
anymore with a digger.
What with BSE, TB and the EEC,

and the shocking weather, she says,
there's no use farming.
And that wind we had last Christmas,
I don't know what it's a sign of,

but we never used to have wind like it.
And the milking parlour
with the new rules and regulations
has to be cleaner than a bathroom,

not even a cobweb.

She takes money for postcards, stamps
and manila envelopes at a blue formica counter,
spotted with freshly spilled blood.

The End of July

The end of July, bunting bullied by the east wind.
A German camper van on the narrow road ahead -
a sign some things have changed.
My father drives with erratic caution,
blasting the horn at each sharp-hedged bend.
I hear my sister's voice from childhood,
'Don't be silly, Daddy, the hedges won't move!'

The red, the white, the blue curbstones
won't budge either and it's a relief
to take the coast road to Cushendall.
The sea is limpid, full of vanishing.
A red trawler hangs in glassy nothingness, its engine throbbing.

We wind down to Murlough Bay, walk to the small cove.
'The McLachlans owned that place,'
Dad points to the cottage on the shore.
'Would you be McLachlans?' he asks a passing couple,
the woman's hair, illuminated tangerine. 'Oh no,' she says,
'we're only down for the day. To watch the birds.'
We all look out to sea and commend the calm.
We say goodbye, watch them walk back. 'People,'
my father says, 'are all right when you speak to them.'
'Yes,' I answer, wondering what itch of predjudice
framed his view. 'Does she dye her hair?'
he asks suddenly. 'Definitely,' I laugh.

He's learnt to suss everything is not as it seems.
I tell him of the night before in a crowded bar,
when a flute-player struck up 'The Sash'

and half the place joined in. One young woman
caught my eye, my closed lips and winked,
'Sure I only learnt it to get past the Prods.'

My father and I decipher Scotland, say little.
We're not a family to name sea campion,
thift, mont bretia, I've learnt all that since,
from books, but he can tell a buzzard treading
air overhead and stretches out his fingers to form wing tips.

He hands me a smoothed round
of basalt, hot with inward heat
drawn from a sun behind thin cloud.
It stays warm until we reach the car.
I know it will become his worry stone,
hope it stores the best of this afternoon:
the seeping milky light, water and sky as one,
all division illusory.

'hot with inward heat' is the name of an Eilis O'Connell sculpture, 1990.

Damian Smyth

Damian Smyth was born in Downpatrick, Co Down, in 1962. He studied Contemporary Philosophy at Queen's University in Belfast. He has edited *All Souls' Night & Other Plays by Joseph Tomelty* (Lagan Press, 1993), *Martin Lynch: Three Plays* (Lagan Press, 1996), *John Hewitt: Two Plays* (Lagan Press, 2000). He has written a play, *Soldiers of the Queen* (nominated for a Stewart Parker Award) and currently works as Arts Development Officer for literature and language arts at the Arts Council of Northern Ireland in Belfast. The poet's two poetry collections are *Downpatrick Races* (Lagan Press, 2000) and *The Down Recorder* (Lagan Press, 2004).

In this poetry the micro-mosaic of Downpatrick intersects with, or implies, wider public and political forces. The poet as townland recorder of lore, real and imagined incidents, tart dialogue or wise-crack, unsaid exchanges, working people's lives and family genealogies is deeply embedded in Irish poetry - but these poems also question (from a contemporary, self-conscious perspective) what it means to record or come from one place as opposed to another. Elegy and memory are key motors: "Of those is our culture. Of those our art. /No one forgotten. Nothing escapes." Discovery is inseparable from recovery here: "Eventually you realise it's all true. /Eventually the dead you never knew /Come to call, one by one, filing through/ Your senses to collect what they are due".
The Down Recorder, a long poem in seven chapters, is based on, and spliced with, stories from this newspaper founded in 1836; it weaves people, place, incident, photography and narrative together to suggest ruptures and parallels - between past and present and between journalism or local history and poetry itself. Factual detail, narratives from particular perspectives, recordings, inclusions, silences and omissions are spliced through a poem which recalls local deaths or history as sources of current love or recurrent pain. Ultimately, there is a sense that ancestry and claimed connection with place over time are an index of connections with elsewhere and everywhere. In the poetry selected from 'The Down Recorder' here the first lines of poems serve as titles.

Tracks

The evening he was blown up by his own bomb at the
        racecourse
he had shaved and showered as though meeting a girlfriend,
Taurus, Brut or Hai Karate sprinkled like myrrh on his talcy body.

Thrown off the scent, neither family nor friends could track him
        at weekends.
But the bomb that woke the birds and set the hurdles blazing
left his bed in the morning unslept in. There was nothing
        in the coffin.

Now each Easter, his name is broadcast by loudspeaker over
        the graveyard,
the wind editing the sentences of the tinny oration
that gives out buckets under the silks of flags and emblems.

On the side of the hill, among the tilting headstones, columns
        of marchers
lean as one into the camber of the uneven ground,
the brassy odour of incense drifting like smoke over the shaven
        heads.

When the breeze brings the tannoy calling the runners and riders
        miles away,
at Binns's big house in the country, where the racecourse
runs for furlongs beside the tarmac road all you hear is bees.

There is the synchronised swimming of starlings and many trees.

The Road to No Town

Don't ask me what any of it means
who walked for miles to find the place it named,

turning back, obeying all the rules
of search and recovery, reading all the signs.

Where land is abandoned by the business of farms
and not a sinner left to tell the tale

then those white sheets hanging out to dry
on the hedges are blackthorn blossom.

The clocks of the tarmac tick in the summer sun
                                    and all the signposts say

the three Irish miles to go are an each way bet,
though everything's in place just as it should be,

as if - as if somewhere here you'd light on what is real,
the shock of something ordinary and safe

to fix the townland fast to its own grave.
A roadway is threaded through the needle's eye of earth

and follows all the contours your maps show,
its grey old back plunging among the hills

with the certainty of purpose tarmac brings.
But the road to Bright is still the road to no town:

a bearing taken, nothing less than that,
a way not *to* or *from* but *in* and *through*.

Butchers

Skeffingtons used cleavers on the meat,
slapping haunches wetly down on wood
and hacking through the bone before your eyes.

Behind the marble altar, in surgeon's gowns,
they rolled out sides of beef like concert harps
and racked up pigs like blazers off the peg.

The butcher's hand was a finger short.
The young would stare at the knuckle's tucked-in skin,
the meat hooks in the window like question marks.

The Celtic Invasions

I

The radio brought Europe close to home,
reining us in by the screaming winches
of airwaves from Madrid and Hilversum
to a continent we could miss by inches,

sweeping the cross-hair over capitals.
The lives lived there were always hours ahead
and at such a pitch we needed aerials
to keep track of the subtle moves they made:

asleep in the afternoon; spaghetti
as white as tapeworms from bad tap water;
words - *confits, confiteor, confetti;*
those rows of skinny people led to slaughter.

It was the war again: *Take that, the Hun!*
Everything learned about Charles de Gaulle,
Sebastian Cabot, the Singing Nun,
the *Dreikaiserbund*, Astérix the Gaul,

falling perfectly into its own place,
old sites of conflict like penalty spots,
the slippery hordes of Holland and Greece
fleeing before the solid Ulster-Scots.

II

I moved men across the green felt map
of *Subbuteo*, like Caesar in his tent
frustrating the French with an off-side trap.
The right move now and those long years spent

inventing victories in small backyards
would come to pass like a new Quattrocento:
a language somehow less than words,
more lasting than bronze or Esperanto:

Dukla Prague, Twente, Dynamo Dresden,
Go Ahead Eagles, Ajax, Bayern Munich,
Eintracht, Utrecht, Parma, St. Etienne,
Ujpest Dozsa, Basle, Grasshoppers Zurich.

Far Out

From Binns's big house, it's miles to the grandstand
where the tannoy fizzles tinily like a bee.
That makes do as a warning
that out of clear skies thunder is coming.

Then it's like nothing is suddenly happening.
The birds stop singing. Grasshoppers cease
flogging their backs, as if watches have stopped.
For down at the turn, thoroughbreds are driving

their clamour ahead of them, flushing the hedgerows
of starlings and fieldmice, ahead of their time.
When the noise and the horses collide where you're standing,
with so much muscle at work under skins,

the eye takes them in like a frieze or mosaic.
It's ecstatic: the animals are carved out of forests,
adrift like galleons with sails of pure silk,
the jockeys scampering high in the rigging.

Out here, where now so much is at stake
it is still massive suffering and cold endurance
on the *Pinto,* the *Niña,* the *Santa Maria,*
that's discovered in binoculars from oceans away.

Fourteen generations laid them down
from Walking Towards Death

Fourteen generations laid them down
to David from Abraham of Ur

and fourteen more from there
to Babylon and on it goes

till every name is named painstakingly
by the tax-collector, crossing every T.

No route is open to us but to drown,
be murdered or be gaoled

or kill ourselves. That's fine.
The young man from the broadsheet

gets it wrong - our names,
our ages, how it all took place

(whatever it was, whatever drew him to,
whatever brought us, predictably at last,

into the universe of what is written down).
He is not to know

how long we've waited for him,
how long hidden out among the world,

disguised as those he knew,
disguised as him.

Our blood still takes him by surprise
though nothing would have made sense otherwise.

Nothing's accidental once it is.

Vacuum
from Walking Towards Death

Vacuum
I said: I am an intimate of ant eater,
blessed at home by its long tropic body.
I give it the room that it needs to turn in
and its sleek snout I guide to dry débris.
Though its ways are gentle, it still gets stuck
in doorways and under chairs, chipping paint.
Its long tongue deals perfectly with spiders,
nostril whistling in the webby corners.

Grateful for blue food behind the cooker
it does not need walked, keeping fit by eating,
and I am fond of the stale heat of its back
and the glad, funny shiverings when full.
House-trained, it shits delicately in bags.
Companion of the loneliest task
you take to your bed awkwardly for days.
When you sleep, you sleep mouth open, standing up.

1987
from Walking Towards Death

Early evening in an empty house.
The paper on the mat brings tardy news
of afternoons spent somewhere in the sun.
Not here for here they have run amok.
What part of Ireland do you come from anyway?
Bodies are coming out of houses in boxes
smuggling technology into the earth -
pacemakers, fillings, artificial hips
as snug as an egg in their soft cardboard pouches
or diaphragms still standing guard at the womb
like boulders that only death can dislodge.
Inside the dead, the plastic is ticking.
All over Ireland lovers are kissing:
the kneecap, the ankle, the elbow, the wrist.

The knives and forks are asleep in the drawer,
the pattern still bright on china plate.
The sofa has moved out. One armchair
hides power points above the skirting board.

Even as we speak it is taking place.
The little electric sex of the light switch
secretly worrying about 'off' and 'on';
slim novels of curtains, half-open, half-closed
and the sun through the window laying
and lifting and swapping its carpet tiles of light.
This is time passing: the screen's cloudy window's
a half-door open on what has gone on
and each afternoon I am miles away
on the terra firma of a chintz armchair,
the miraculous distance of a medieval saint
spotted on two different continents at once.
Here. There. Nowhere. Everywhere.

It is a distraction, the light at St John's Point
from Salt

It is a distraction, the light at St John's Point.
In the silence, the sound of the mirrors turning
in daylight already assures the destination of the
    light at night -
a mechanism tremendous and accurate, its tremors
sent down into the earth through its funnel of
    stone,
blades carving the air in the white face of the bulb
as if there's a lunatic up there fighting the sun with
    a pitchfork.

It is not that. It is not that.
from Salt

It is not that. It is not that
the steel axe was better made than the stone.
It is not that they thought less well
or with less accuracy than us.
Or with less confusion and error
when the need arose to be confused and wrong.
They dealt as well as us but with different things,
most often every day with the treachery of the
    obvious
because they were simply more naked to it
and not sheltered from it as fully as us:
how far-off things still stubbornly appear much
    smaller,
much less careful that what is prejudiced by being
    near.

Andy White

Andy White was born in Belfast in 1962. He read English at Robinson College, Cambridge, and has been writing and recording music, releasing numerous albums since 1985. Andy White's collection of poetry and song is entitled *The Music of What Happens* (Lagan Press, 1998).

The work of Andy White is characterised by short, instantly accessible lyrics akin to popular songs or found poems. While the poems, based in popular musical traditions, give rise to the question of whether they exist independently of sung performance these short fragments and ballads have both an instantaneous life that gives rise to futher questions or implications. The poem-songs are akin to speedy jottings or notes left by someone on the move, a street sketch by Jacques Prevert or a small still-life by William Carlos Williams. The work has a condensed humour and honesty so that what is lost in layering or depth in poetry as song is gained in resonance and spontaneous impact. Indeed the poems reflect on Belfast's poetic pretensions which, like Napoli's musical ones, are often punctured by the reality of its own streets: "Outside in the street/bit of bother/people hurling/ anthologies at each other". Similiarly prose, which often takes itself too seriously, is the target in 'Two novelists in search of an argument' which rewrites the proverb, perhaps ironically, as "the pen is mightier than the words".

The street symphony of Napoli

If I could write
the street symphony
of Napoli
it would start with you walking into
that Italian bar
if I could write
the street symphony of Napoli
it would be played by a
thousand ruined cars

dilapidated
beyond repair
their horns blaring

never in time
never in tune
and the score would be
stolen from my hotel room

Hey man, there's an Ulster poet
in the hotel lobby

Ulster poet
seated
on location
on commission
slim volumes
thing past

Suddenly
Cuchulain and his
axe
swing into Reception

lights up a Gallaher's blue
the poet fondles his
pen
'Leave me alone' shouts Cuch
'I'm immortalised already
Give me peace
whoojoo think y'are
Louis Macfuckingneice?
Don't drag me into a poem
I'm averse to it.'

Outside in the street
bit of bother
people hurling
anthologies at each other

Before the big rain

You tied up all the artists
and really made them think
with your cinematic profile
and your heart in the clink

you opened a café for the
children from the west
who'd flown in specially
at the poet's request

it was a night I can't remember
those are the nights
I remember you best
but I can still recall
you had a visionary name
and the streetcorner girls
were singing 'Sweet Jane'
before the big rain

Cornmarket in December

They're selling christmas on the streets
10p a sheet 10p a sheet

One

The government of love
has increased its majority
by one

Christine holding on
and pushing out

and now
Sebastian
is lying serious beside her

and the government of love
has increased its majority
by one

The concert has not been a success

after Jacques Prevert

The concert has not been a success,
and everybody knows it.
Although it's hard to say out loud,
I see it in the laundered faces
and counterfeit glances
gathering at the bar.

companions in these bad days,
remember the evenings it worked.

now I will get
something to eat
something to drink.
I have my guitars
and two or three cigarettes
left in the packet.

the concert has not been a success.
Companions in these bad days
I wish you good night.

Two novelists in search of an argument

They try football and
cricket and
poets and persons and
dinner and discos and dancing and
cigarettes and beer
but the pen is mightier than the
words
and they end up quite near to
kissing and hugging and

whispering opening paragraphs
in each others' ears.

Losing Lives

Compromise is losing lives
so the radio told me so

The dictatorship of rhyme

It happens all the time

The sound of no helicopters

Peace
sounds like
the sound of no helicopters

previous
city of car blasts
is strangely quiet
because
peace sounds like
the sound of no helicopters

Sabine Wichert

Sabine Wichert was born in Graudenz, West Prussia (now Grudziadz, Poland) in 1942 and grew up in West Germany. Educated at various German and English universities, she has taught history at Queen's University, Belfast, since 1971. Her poetry collections are *Tin Drum Country* (Salmon Publishing, 1995), *Sharing Darwin* (Salmon Publishing, 1999) and *Taganrog* (Lagan Press, 2004).

This poetry encompasses European and Irish history and moves, geographically, between the domesticities of an adopted home in Northern Ireland and the complex legacies of central and eastern Europe. The poetry balances impersonal, often overwhelming forces (the when and where of history) and personal perspectives (views from a here and now) to reveal that the personal and historical are enmeshed. Poems weigh emotional commitment and intellectual detachment in the balance and in the full awareness that, historically speaking, survival is often dependent on neither - but on flight or keeping your head down. The poetry is deeply aware of history - its impact in redrawn maps or scars left in the psyche: 'Of Lagan and Vistula' reflects on rivers on the same latitude where "people glanced /over their shoulder/before confirming/nationhood in blood and soil". Certainty and uncertainty oscillate in a poem like 'The Gate' which is equally wary of both open and closed doors; the poem suggests that poetry deals not just with metaphors or symbols but with flight or enclosure as historical realities. In more recent poems there is a focus on the contours of inner or emotional worlds; relationships, the warm intimacies and claustrophobic fears that friends, family and lovers bring, are a burden, romantic interlude, an alleviation of solitude - which make "life more difficult, / but living easier".

Of Vistula and Lagan

When I was born
they had just
liberated the land
from alien possession.
Where I was born
ownership of land
was much disputed.

I inherited
the burning cities
of Europe,
the pulped flesh
and distorted minds,
and always
the marching boots:
mine, mine, mine.

When I was born
my father's name
had just
been changed
to sound more German.
Where I was born
nations were at war.

Human material
was in vogue,
skin cheap,
people glanced
over their shoulder
before confirming
nationhood
in blood and soil.

So I learnt
that names
don't matter,
and land
doesn't belong,
that roots grow
in many soils,

and power
is dangerous
in any hand,
politician's,
priest's or poet's;
that many rivers
flow across
one latitude.

Irish Summer

Sometimes
it smells of summer
even here,
when the wind is right
and the rain
not too heavy:
rose-petals and lavender
among the heathers,
and if you are quiet
you can hear
the bog singing
of tree-times
and butterflies.

The Gate

I ponder half-baked philosophies:
to be or not to be a sheep:

instinct and herd
versus insight and individual,

while two little boys
practice their dexterity:

for half an hour they close
and open the gate

never losing a moment's
interest or intense concentration.

I'm not so certain either
whether it's better open or shut;

and after half a life-time's practice
I still don't trust doors
half-closed or half-open.

The Smell of Frying Cheese

Sometimes she woke to the noise of soldiers
and the alien smell of frying cheese.
They'd bivouac under the ancient trees
by the side of the dirt-road. Those oaks
almost saw Napoleon, it was said,
but he didn't quite make it this way. The war
was over, but the locals remained

suspicious. They did not like this freedom -
bringing British soldiers with their gibberish
and gypsies' ways. You could not trust what was
not yours. She, too, had learned to be cautious,
curious, careful, alert and ready
to run as she had had to with her parents

from faraway places bowing to
the patterns of centuries: if you can,
move on. The natives had stayed put, kept their
heads down and survived. By now the soldiers
paid for their eggs, chicken and milk; they had

brought freedom, they said, but no food. Neither
were heroes or rebels watching each other
with beady eyes. By then she had also learnt
to respect but never trust uniforms.

She left before she was quite one of them
and often thought of ancient oaks, the smell
of frying cheese, the need to survive and move on.

Laying Poison

The old, unevenly lettered, hand-painted rusty
board, POISON LAYED, at the gate to the field has
been replaced by a shiny new plastic and professionally
printed one: Beware of Cross Fresian Bull. Enter
at your own risk.

After your visit to the golden wedding in Strabane,
where unemployment pushes against and meets
the border, your watercolours dissolved into reality.

More deadly, civilisations without wars?
The indeterminable breakdown. But of what?

Sitting around the master table somewhere: strategy
and tactics: how to employ their forces, which hills
to take, which villages to clear, how many buildings
to eliminate and which people to cleanse.

Mapping death and destruction:
why maps were invented, what we are about.

October

Don't meet or mate, they say,
when the apples have ripened,
no new seed will germinate,
you've left it too late for nature.

But then, you can always defy
them: be human, have spring
or summer in autumn or
winter: no need to multiply.

Coriander in the Rain

Shiny bright fruit growing high
on trees, always out of reach.
They hardly throw a shadow.

Your urge to devour the exotic:
green chillies, coriander and
turmeric; then later coconut,
pawpaw and guava, mango,
orange, kiwi and quinces.

What you cannot eat you try
to remember: magnolia,
orchids and bougainvillaea;
the exuberance of colours
defying imagination: jasmine,
amaryllis and granadilla.

For one day soon you'll have
to go home again to Sunday
roasts with two dull veg
and a summer pudding at best.
Do you hear the rain waiting for you?

Play It Again

Swifts darting from underneath the crown
of the big beech, gliding over the fields,
getting their feed open-mouthed, to and fro,
danger to insects, image of freedom.

Now I stir as I watch them, when I
think of the years of false trust and lying;
the usual sting: the eyes always had
it - this time they are brown, of the deep, dark
chocolate variety: at one glance

the Casablanca syndrome: still lurking,
half-forgotten. His malt, my red wine, heat;
being strangers, strange together in a
strange place: possibly war and resistance,
certainly adventure and romantic
illusion: claustrophobic and cloying,

freedom, liberation; also perhaps
primeval: the urge to couple before
the doom, translated into undying
passion, unfulfillable love. Shadows
falling between meeting and matching. But
play it again - for the memory, and
the darting swifts, the softly falling rain.

Eternity in Taganrog
found poem

The eternal flame burning
in the Russian city of Taganrog
to honour those killed
in the Second World War
went out after the city
failed to pay its gas bill.

The Site of Railway Tracks in Co. Sligo

Only the map's imagination sees
tracks of the railway branch line between Kilfree
Junction and Ballaghaderreen, where fences,
brambles and nettles bar my way; there is
nothing left but the site of what once connected
people and enticed further afield.

Then there were cattle trains on tracks criss-crossing
Europe, Jews being travelled one way, a little
later refugees took the opposite route,
and most of *us* survived the journey.

And finally the English couple, holding
up the queue at the luggage x-ray machine
in Vienna's airport lounge, moved on, feeling

hustled and frail: 'He said the knife was pointed.
Of course it was pointed', and he replied
'I suppose once they get suspicious they
look at everything, which isn't fair, really.'